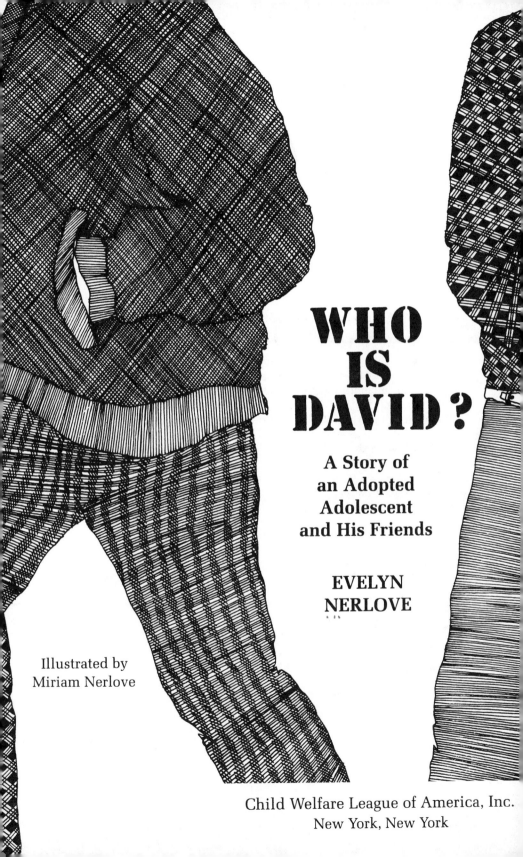

WHO IS DAVID?

A Story of an Adopted Adolescent and His Friends

EVELYN NERLOVE

Illustrated by
Miriam Nerlove

Child Welfare League of America, Inc.
New York, New York

F
N357 W

CHILD WELFARE LEAGUE OF AMERICA, INC.
67 Irving Place, New York, 10003

Current printing (last digit)
10 9 8 7 6 5 4 3 2 1

Printed in the United States of America

Library of Congress Cataloging in Publication Data

Nerlove, Evelyn A.
   Who is David?

   Summary: By attending a children's service bureau
workshop, David meets other adopted teenagers and
comes to terms with his identity as an adopted child.
   [1. Adoption—Fiction] I. Title.
PZ7.N43775Wh 1985   [Fic]   85-3837
ISBN 0-87868-233-3

Designed by Joan Stoliar

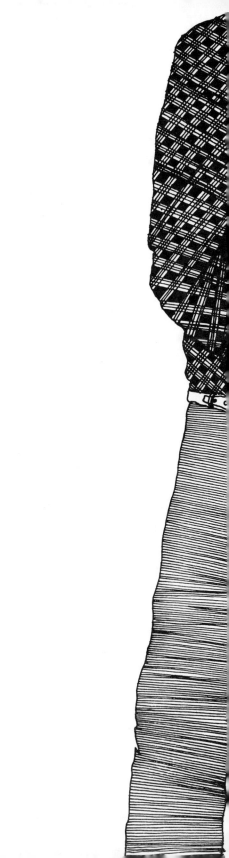

David Brooks

stirred in his sleep. Then

he heard the sound of muffled footsteps, as if someone were creeping

stealthily up the stairs. The footsteps came closer and closer. The door to his bedroom opened slowly, soundlessly. A black-masked figure leapt into the room, threw a blanket over his head, grabbed him, then crept back down the stairs. David screamed and kicked, but the black-masked figure held him in a vise-like grip.

David awoke with a start. Who was the black-masked figure? Who would want to steal him?

Sometimes during this dream he awoke, screaming and kicking the blankets away, crying "HELP! HELP!"

Whenever this happened, his mother and father rushed into his room. Even with his mom's arms around him, David still could not stop his sobs. He was aware of his dad just standing there, looking annoyed and uncertain. How strange it was to see Dad looking like that! Dad, who was so powerful, so definite and sure of himself when he was giving orders and advice.

When at last he could control his fear, David lay back exhausted. His parents left the room. They always left his door and theirs open after these nightmares.

Although he was half-asleep, David could still hear them talking. Sometimes he could hear his mother's voice, saying, "Troubled." And his father answering, "Worried . . ."

His mom and dad had told him that he had been adopted through an agency. Adoption agencies did not buy babies or sell them—*he knew that.* But how did the agency get him? And why did Mom and Dad talk about "finding" him? Did that mean someone had "lost" him? Or had just not wanted him and had thrown him away?

But not his mom and dad, *never!* Mom and Dad would never have lost him or given him away. Mom was always talking about how much she had wanted a baby, how much she had wanted *him.*

"And that's why we adopted you," she would say. "How lucky we were to have found you!"

David must have been about six years old when his mom had first told him that she and his dad had not been able to make a baby of their own. "We had needed you so much and you needed us."

That was the hard part to understand. Why should he have needed them, if he had been born in the regular way? He despaired of ever knowing the truth. The stories Mom and Dad told him were too difficult to understand. "The man and woman who gave birth to you loved you and wanted you to have a good home, with two parents."

As the years passed, David came to know children who didn't have two parents. So what had been wrong with *him* that he could not have stayed with *one* parent, if that had been the reason why he had to be adopted.

These thoughts became a torment to David by the time he reached thirteen years of age. It got worse when he told Alex Parsons that he was adopted. Alex was a new boy who had moved into the neighborhood and was in the eighth grade with him.

"Adopted!" Alex repeated, shocked. "Yuck! You mean your REAL mother gave you away? You mean Jonathan and Laura Brooks are not your *real* parents?"

David had been too hurt to tell his mother about that

one. He remembered with anguish the time he was five and had told Jimmy, who lived next door, that he was adopted. Jimmy wondered if he, too, had been adopted. It seemed a nice thing to be, the way David said it.

"I'm going to ask my mom if I was adopted," Jimmy had said.

The next morning, when Jimmy came out to play with David, the first thing he said was, "I'm lucky. My mom and dad were able to make their own babies. They didn't have to get me from someone else who 'borned' me."

What in the world could Jimmy have meant by that?

"My mom and dad could make their own babies," Jimmy repeated proudly. "And they could keep me. Yours had to give you away. That means you have *two* mothers."

Two mothers! The way Jimmy said it, it sounded like something bad, like having two heads, or green hair, or six fingers on each hand.

David had run into the house, crying.

"Mom, do I have two mothers?"

His mother's face had turned red, and she looked angry. "Of course not," she said in a kind of choked voice. "I'm your mother, your only mother. Who's been telling you things like that?"

"That's what Jimmy's mom told him." David remembered feeling anxious, even a little frightened.

"Well, I'll have to have a talk with her." His mother's voice was still angry, but her face looked sad. She had read David the story of adoption ever since he was three or four years old. She told him the story again, and then he understood that the baby in the story was himself, but it had all been confusing. He didn't like to remember seeing his mom sad, so he pushed it out of his mind.

But now, at thirteen, he had read many science books. They fascinated him. He learned that things that happen to a person leave "creases" in the memory part of the brain, and that they are there for the rest of your life. Most of the time a person doesn't even think about them, or know that deep down he "remembers" them.

David let his mind wander back in time, thinking of

5

many things he had suppressed over the years. At bedtime, alone with his thoughts, he tossed and turned and tried to recall how he had come to understand what adoption really meant.

When he finally fell into a fitful sleep, he dreamed the same dream that often recurred—the horror of being snatched from his bed by a masked figure. Those nights were torture to him, and even in broad daylight he was filled with pain and confusion when he recalled the dream.

One morning after one of these nightmares, David asked his parents when they had first told him about his being adopted.

"Our social worker, Mrs. Nelson, advised us to use the word right from the beginning, dear," his mother told him, "so that you would know that adoption was something good. It was to be a word that would never frighten you, or cause you to feel hurt in any way."

"I used to call you 'my darling adopted boy' when I bathed you, dressed you, and cuddled you," she continued.

His father looked up from the paper he was reading. David was always surprised when his father, seemingly preoccupied with the morning newspaper, joined the conversation at breakfast.

"When I rolled a ball to you, long before you could catch it," Dad said, "I would call out to you, 'This is for my strong adopted son!'"

"No wonder I always felt different," David muttered.

"You're everything I always hoped for in a son—strong and brave."

His dad was in great spirits that morning. It always made David feel good when his parents talked that way about wanting him and loving him.

"You know what I remember? I remember Grandma Lola describing how I used to play with that toy doctor's kit she gave me when I was little. She told me I used to parade around the house with the ends of the stethoscope in my ears, saying, 'I'm a doptor . . . I'm a doptor.' And Grandma said everyone always knew that was what I thought being adopted meant. People always laughed, so I kept repeating it."

David paused, his brow furrowed with the effort of remembering. "I guess that's why I thought being adopted was so great that I kept telling people about it.

"But I don't tell people any more. Most of them act so funny about it. Either they ask me a whole lot of questions, like, How come? Or they look sad or surprised or uncomfortable. Some of the kids tell me about some baby being left at a bus station, or in a garbage can. They ask if that happened to me!"

"Oh dear," his mother said. His dad cleared his throat. David stopped talking. He felt mean saying all those things that made his parents feel sad. But he also felt something else, a kind of satisfaction in hurting them. After all, they had taken him away from his "real" parents, hadn't they?

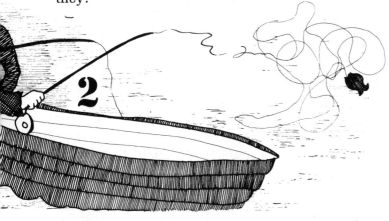

The summer after David turned thirteen, his father took him on a fishing trip for a whole week. Just the two of them. They looked forward to having a great time together.

"And now that you're so grown up, David," his father said to him, "why don't you call me J.B.?"

"Thanks, J.B. I like that!"

They rented a boat at a place by a lake and bought

fishing tackle and drinks to go with the sandwiches they had brought from home.

The day was filled with long silences as they waited for the jerk of the line. "Wow, J.B., look!" David whispered as he finally felt a tug on his line.

David would always remember the rush of the water and the struggle of the fish and how his father encouraged him to reel in his catch. Or sometimes it was David who watched breathlessly while his father brought in a fish. What compliments and admiration they showed for each other's successes!

"Great, David! You did it, you did it! That took a lot of strength!

David felt terrific when his father praised him like that. His chest puffed out. He felt like a man in his dad's own world, someone his dad was proud of.

They ate each day's catch by the fire. Food never tasted so good. After they ate, they stretched out, or took a walk around the lake. Then they got ready to bed down in their sleeping bags.

This was a time for them to be together, a chance for them to talk. David longed to tell his father what the nightmares that he had been having were like, how frightened they made him, the thoughts that came into his mind when he awoke. In fact, David suspected that his mother just might have urged this father-son vacation so that David might have a good opportunity to do just that. This arrangement was typical of the way his mother did things. She was tactful, and he was grateful to her, but he still had hurt feelings.

As far back as David could remember, he was always closer to his mother than to his father, more comfortable with her. It seemed only recently that she had stopped the night-time play ritual that he would remember all his life . . . the finger games . . . "this little piggy went to market . . ." stuff like that. And the stretching of each arm, the pull of each leg as she would say, "Oh, how you are growing . . . stretch, stretch . . . grow, grow . . ."

He remembered also his mother's pride when, as they

stood before the mirror after his daily bath, she would say, "When I was little and my hair was as red as yours, and I had freckles like yours, I hated it. I wanted to have brown eyes and black hair like my friend Angela. But now I have a handsome son with red hair and freckles, and I wish my hair were still as red as yours is now. And now I'm glad that I have freckles, although yours are lots bigger than mine and I love them like that! I'm glad that we both have blue eyes, and those won't change."

Another reason he was closer to his mother was that she had always understood him best. When things weren't going right, she seemed to know. She comforted him without prying too much. But OK! He was getting to be pretty big for that kind of stuff. A boy ought to be close to his father. But something kept David from blurting out what he really wanted to talk about. Instead, he said, "You know what, J.B.? I hope I can get to be a professor, like you."

His dad's face lit up. "That's the best compliment a son can give his father."

So far, so good, David thought. Maybe he could still work around to what he had on his mind.

"Of course you know, David, that you're going to have to work hard in school."

"I know. My teachers think I'm OK."

There was a long pause. David still didn't have the courage to ask his father what he really wanted to know.

"Dad, remember when you used to take me to your office on a Saturday or Sunday, when you dropped off some papers or looked for a book? I sure liked that you took me along and let me write on the blackboard. Remember?"

"Yes, I do, as a matter of fact. I remember how good you were about not disturbing me, or asking me a whole lot of questions when I was trying to concentrate on my work. I'm sure you would have liked to, right?"

"Yeah, but I knew you were too busy." David vividly recalled how anxious he had been to please his father, how hopeless he had felt about being able to get close to him. He still felt that way.

"You know, J.B., that's when I first thought I wanted

to be a professor, like you. It must be interesting. I'd like to know more about it."

That started his father talking about his work, the book he was writing, and the classes in economics that he was teaching at UCLA. His father told him that there were different theories that were supposed to solve world economic problems—and each theory was connected with some important professor or scholar who had written about each. His father mentioned the names of Karl Marx, Thorsten Veblen, Joan Robinson . . . Keynes . . . Pigou . . . Friedman.

David listened eagerly, and his father didn't notice that David didn't understand most of what he had been talking about.

Still, everything considered, it was a terrific trip. It was fun. And he felt closer to his dad than he ever had felt before. Almost chummy.

Yet he wasn't able to get up the courage to ask his dad about what was on his mind until his father finally gave him the chance.

"David, do you have something you wanted to talk with me about?"

"Well, J.B. . . . ." How could he say it? Angry with himself, vaguely realizing the fear within him, he blurted out, "I was thinking about the other lady who adopted me out . . . I mean my *real* mother. I wonder why she gave me away."

David felt his cheeks growing red. His voice trembled. He was angry with himself for not being able to keep calm. But at last it was out in the open, the question that had been festering in his mind. He needed desperately to find the answer.

Jonathan Brooks cleared his throat. He straightened up and looked a little stiff. David wondered if that was the way his father looked when he was lecturing in one of the classes he taught. Then he spoke.

His words came out slowly and carefully. "David, being a mother doesn't depend on a woman being able to

10

grow a baby inside her. It means loving and caring for a child. We took you into our home and loved you as if you were our own. I mean you ARE ours, of course, our very own, and no one else's. Mother and I are your parents . . ."

There was a pause. It was clear to David that his father was having a hard time answering the question about why his "real" parents had given him away.

Strange! This was not his father, the Professor, that David had always pictured in his mind's eye, talking with his colleagues or students, or lecturing to his classes.

When at last he spoke, the words came out slowly. "David, the woman who gave birth to you and the man— uh . . ." There was a long pause while his father tried to find just the right words. Then he continued as if he knew exactly what he wanted to say.

"The man who was responsible for your coming into the world, and the woman who gave birth to you, were never able to take care of you, so you became ours. We went to court to make it legal, so that no one would ever take you away from us.

"The man and woman who were your biological—I mean your *birth* parents—were never your parents in any real sense. They were not able to take care of you, so they did the next best thing. They arranged for you to have parents who could love you and give you a good home."

David thought his father looked relieved and rather pleased with himself. But David's thoughts were angry and bitter.

Yeah, the next best thing, he thought. He was supposed to be grateful for having a good home. But he still wanted to know who that other man and woman were, and why they couldn't have taken care of him.

The more David thought about it, the more he felt that something must have been wrong with him. Otherwise, why would his REAL mother and father have given him away?

11

David's anger grew and grew, but he kept it inside. It frightened him to be so angry. His fear made him angrier. The angrier he became, the more frightened he was. I mustn't think of it any more, he told himself. I MUST put it out of my mind!

He told himself he had to think of something pleasant. The thought of his friend, Diana, came to his mind. He could tell *her* anything.

By the time they arrived home, David was feeling better. He gave his mother a terrific hug. She asked him a million questions about the fishing, and he told her all about it. He showed her the big trout they had carefully brought home packed in ice bought at a little tackle shack.

His father was in a good mood, too. And David tried to make sure that his mother did not suspect how angry and disappointed he was feeling.

3

Diana Woods and David had been in the same grade in school since kindergarten. David passed Diana's house every morning on the way to school, and they walked together the rest of the way. It flattered David to suspect that sometimes Diana waited for him before she came out of her doorway. He had always felt easy in her company. He liked to look at her. She had a pretty way of tossing her head, so that her long blonde hair sometimes touched his shoulders, and he loved to hear her quick laughter, which came so easily and so often. Her brown eyes sparkled when she laughed, and his own grew moist when he laughed with her.

The Brooks family and the Woods family were friendly, especially the mothers. They exchanged recipes and gave each other tips on the care of gardens and other household matters. But in other ways the two women were different. Florence Woods was an outgoing woman who was active in local politics. Her husband, George Woods, was a partner in a large, well-known firm specializing in corporate law. They had a large home and lived more lavishly than the Brooks family.

David's mother was an artist who was beginning to gain recognition for her portraits. To supplement the family income, Laura Brooks worked part-time at a local art museum, but she was always home to send David off to school and to welcome him when he returned.

David was attracted to art, and he used to like to play in his mother's tiny attic studio while she painted. A work of David's even hung in his parents' bedroom. It was a composition of odd shapes and splashes of color that David had painted when he was seven. He often amused himself by creating Klee-like images on sheets of paper his mother gave him.

Then something happened right in his own territory that further awakened David's confusion and anger about his birth. It was common gossip in the neighborhood and at school that Diana's sister, Emily, had become pregnant in her sophomore year in high school. And she didn't give *her* baby away! She and Bruce, her baby, lived at home. Mrs. Woods took care of Bruce during the hours that Emily was at school, with some help from a maid who came in daily. Diana didn't talk much about her sister, but David was curious and one day he asked her a lot of questions about the baby.

"Diana, I hear that the baby in your house is really Emily's. Is that true?"

"Where did you hear that?" Diana's voice held a note of anger.

"I heard some of the boys talking about it at lunchtime. Is it true?"

"Yes, it is. But I hate to have people talking about it. My parents are very angry with Jack Ross for getting Emily pregnant."

"Why did she let him . . . you know?" David asked, annoyed with himself when he felt his face reddening.

Diana smiled in a motherly kind of way. David thought she must be thinking he was pretty straight, not being able to say the words.

"Jack was eighteen and should have known better than to get a fifteen-year-old girl pregnant. Jack's parents wanted Emily to put the baby up for adoption, but my parents said he was our flesh and blood, and they told Emily that they would help her take care of the baby."

"Does Emily like the baby?"

"Some of the time she likes him, but she gets angry when he cries. My parents make her stay home a lot, too, and she would rather go out and have fun."

David often thought about Emily and her baby. He tried to picture himself in the baby's place.

One time David saw Emily in the park giving the baby some beer to drink! And another time Emily forgot to put the brake on the baby's carriage while she was talking to Ken Owens in the park. The carriage started to roll downhill, and Emily didn't even notice! She was busy laughing with Ken.

Would he have liked someone like Emily for a mother?

Especially since he discovered that Emily had had a baby, there were many times that David wanted to ask his parents about his birth mother and father, but he felt uncomfortable with just the thought of asking. One evening on the six o'clock news, which his mom and dad liked to watch together, there was a report about a little baby boy who had

14

been found early one morning in the washroom at Union Station downtown.

David looked up sharply from the self-portrait he was sketching with the new charcoals his mother had bought him. The cleaning man who found the baby was saying that the baby's diaper was soaking wet. The baby also must have cried a lot and been hungry, because the upper part of his shirt and the blanket around him were all wet and looked as if he might have been sucking on them.

David thought of all the things that could have happened to make someone leave a baby and go away "just like that!"

"Was that baby bad?" he asked his mother.

"Oh, no!" she answered. "Babies aren't ever *bad*. They may be sick or hungry, and cry for attention or food and care. Babies need to be cuddled and loved. But babies are never BAD! No, indeed!"

His father said, "Maybe the mother figured she just couldn't take care of him and thought he'd be better off if she left him somewhere he was sure to be found—as, in fact, he was. She knew that good care would be given him, the kind of care that she probably wasn't able to provide."

"It isn't easy to give up a baby," his mom said. "Sometimes a mother is depressed and desperate, and doesn't know where to turn."

David began to watch the newspapers to see what he could learn about other children who had been abandoned. It was rare, he noticed, that babies were abandoned. But there were other reports in the news that really scared him. Some children had been physically abused—beaten, thrown downstairs or against walls—horrible things! He also came across some reports of children who had been sexually molested. What could that mean?

He wondered what had really happened when he was a baby, and couldn't help feeling, despite what his mother and father had said, that something had been wrong with him, that he was somehow no good.

15

4

The year that David turned fourteen was full of changes. He entered high school. He grew four inches in height and developed broad shoulders. Hair began to grow under his arms, around his penis and on his upper lip.

"I'm going to have to get you a razor and show you how to use it," his father said, rather proudly.

David's voice had also begun to change in the past year. At times it was deep. At other times it broke into high notes. He was embarrassed when that happened, and if he thought about it beforehand, he hesitated to talk at all. It was always worse when he was called on in class, and sometimes he pretended not to know the answer.

He even began to act differently toward his mother. He stopped kissing her at night before going to bed. When she asked him to do an errand, or some chore around the house, he sometimes deliberately pretended not to hear her.

"David," she said one day, "didn't you hear me?" Her voice could be really sharp when she was impatient. "You forgot to take out the trash last night after dinner."

David's answer was to turn up the sound on the TV.

"David, did you hear me?" She came closer. "Don't forget to take out the trash tonight, do you hear?"

"Yeah, I hear you. You don't have to yell at me."

"I do if you don't answer me. How do I know that you hear me if you don't answer?"

David got up slowly. He pushed past her, so close that if she hadn't moved aside he would have bumped straight into her.

16

"David!" she shouted. "What do you mean by acting this way?"

"Hell," he muttered, half to himself, but loud enough for her to hear. "I can talk to you any way that I like. You're not my *real* mother."

"I am so your real mother."

"You *bought* me!"

"David!" she screamed. "What in the world has gotten into you? 'Bought you!' What kind of talk is that?"

When David returned from taking out the trash he heard the voices of his parents as they talked behind the closed door of their bedroom. David couldn't make out the words, although he put his ear to the door.

They're talking about me, he thought. *I really shook Mom up!* He gloated. He was glad to hurt her, but part of him was sad and sorry.

That night he thought of them together in bed. He had begun to think of them that way now and then. It made him feel alone and unhappy.

Sometimes he wished that he were little again. He remembered all the nice things about being little—the hugs, the games, the laughter, and Mom and Dad on the floor with him, David—all their attention on HIM! But the more he wished that he were little again, the more unpleasant he became. Often he went to bed without saying goodnight. Then he would turn on his radio at full blast, on purpose. His parents would come in holding their hands to their ears. He felt a kind of joy as one of them turned off his radio and scolded him.

David's nightmares were worse after such episodes.

That year David fell in love with Ms. Martin, his French teacher. He had always enjoyed French class. He just loved the sound of the language. But even when Ms. Martin spoke English, he loved hearing her talk. She always put the stress on the last syllable. For instance, she called him DavEED. He knew that Ms. Martin considered him a good student, and he responded to her by working hard and giving her his full attention.

But one day in class, as he was listening to her explaining some point in grammar, he found himself more interested in her than in what she was saying. She was all brightness and movement. Her eyes and teeth sparkled when she smiled. Head, hands, shoulders—everything moved as she talked in that quick, light way of hers.

David wondered if his birth mother was anything like Ms. Martin. Was she French? He couldn't remember what his parents had told him about his birth mother's nationality, but he hoped that she was French. He fantasized that some day she would explain everything to him—how she came to give birth to him, why she gave him up, who he really was.

"Dav—EED!" The sound of his name startled him into attention. "Please answer the question, DavEED," Ms. Martin said, a puzzled look on her face.

What had she asked? He tried to pull himself together. No way! He blew it—and the whole class and Ms. Martin knew it!

Diana and David were in the same French class, and Diana was waiting for him outside the classroom that day.

"Did you bring your lunch today?" she asked.

"Yeah."

"I'm starving. Let's eat."

They sat on the grass munching their sandwiches and gulping their milk from their thermos bottles. David wondered why Diana was looking at him so disapprovingly.

"David, did you tell Alex Parsons that you were adopted?"

"Yeah, what about it?" David was relieved. He would have felt foolish if Diana were to suspect that he had been daydreaming about Ms. Martin.

"Why did you tell *him*? That was silly! What did he say?"

"He said, 'Yuck! You mean your real mother gave you

away? Your parents didn't want you?' Why are you asking, Diana?"

"Alex is telling all the kids at school that your real mother didn't want you and didn't even know who your father was. He says she dumped you in a garbage can in the parking lot of a liquor store, and that when the police found you they turned you over to the County. And also . . ." Diana suddenly stopped, her face was flushed and her lip trembled.

"And also what?" David couldn't keep his voice firm and calm, as he would have liked.

Diana hesitated. "Well . . . Alex says the reason you don't have a Walkman or your own TV set is because your parents don't care enough about you to give them to you. He always brags about the stuff his parents give him. I think he's stupid."

David shrugged. But it was true. His parents couldn't give him all the things his friends had. Why do I have to be different, he thought. Why can't we be rich, like most of the families around here? Why couldn't Mom and Dad have had me like other people have children?

Diana must have read his thoughts. "Maybe you're lucky, David. Emily's baby would be better off if he were adopted. Emily's always slapping and scolding him when my mother or the maid aren't around. Emily'd rather play with dolls, I think—and so does my mother!—than take care of a real live baby like Bruce who gets into things when he shouldn't, and gets hungry and tired, and cries."

"Well, I don't know, Diana. I wish I hadn't had to be adopted. I wish I knew what my REAL mother and father were like. I wish I could see them. I wish I knew why they gave me away."

Wish, wish, wish, that's all I can do, David thought.

"David, there must have been a good reason. You're great just the way you are. You really are. And you're not stupid, like some of the other boys."

I wish I were like the other boys, David thought.

5

One day after school, feeling famished, David went to the refrigerator to get a snack. He found a bright, orange-colored paper attached to the door by a magnet, the way his mother did when she wanted to remember something. The heading at the top was in large letters:

WORKSHOPS FOR YESTERDAY'S
AND TODAY'S
ADOPTIVE FAMILIES

David took the notice down and sat at the table with it. He cut himself a slice of cheese and poured out a tall glass of grapefruit juice. As he ate, he read:

We are offering a Workshop for parents and adoles-
cent adoptees. You will have an opportunity to
meet with other families who share interests and
concerns similar to yours.

David was too excited to read the rest of it. He tried to be nonchalant as he climbed the stairs to his mother's studio. He didn't care to have her know how excited he was about getting to know other kids who were adopted.

His mother didn't even hear him come in, she was so immersed in her painting. He cleared his throat, made a scraping sound with a chair, and said, "Er-a–I read the notice about the group they're having at the Children's Bureau."

He waited a second, and wasn't surprised when his mother said, "Uh-huh?" David knew she wasn't listening whenever she said "Uh-huh" that way, with a preoccupied air.

"Dammit, Mom! You aren't listening!" He practically screamed the words. He hated it when she did that to him.

His mother shook herself and turned away from the canvas she was painting. "I'm sorry, dear," she said. "You know how I am when I get into my work."

"Yeah, but I wish you'd pay attention to me when I talk." David thought he sounded a lot like his father when he used that firm, "bossy" kind of voice.

His mother looked a little surprised. David knew she didn't like him to talk that way to her. Sometimes when he screamed at her because she wasn't listening, she'd say, "Stop being such a tyrant!"

To avoid her anger, even though most of the time David got a kick out of making her feel in the wrong, he changed the subject.

"What are you painting, Mom?"

"An abstract."

David noticed that on the floor beside her was a reproduction of a painting of a mother holding a baby. It looked like a copy of something very old, that might be hanging in a museum.

"What is that? Who painted it?" he asked.

"It's Bellini's *Madonna and Child*."

"Why do you keep it there?"

"Because it's so beautiful. It gives me inspiration."

"It really does inspire you, doesn't it? See? Your abstract has some of the shape of the woman and her baby."

His mother looked startled. She was staring with amazement at the canvas she had been painting.

"Why, David, I believe you're right."

She looked at David with a puzzled expression. Then

21

with a sudden smile she dropped her paintbrush and hugged him.

"Mom . . ." David hesitated. Why was it so hard to mention the Adoption Workshop?

"I saw the announcement on the refrigerator."

"Oh, yes." She looked at David questioningly, but he said nothing.

"Do you think you might be interested, David?"

"Oh, I don't know . . ." He tried to sound casual and kind of indifferent. "Do you and Dad plan to go?"

"Yes, we're very much interested. We signed up for ourselves. The first four meetings are for the parents only. Then the meetings for the children begin."

David eagerly looked forward to meeting other adopted kids. The evening that his parents left for the first meeting, he found himself unable to concentrate on his homework. Nor could he watch television. He even went to bed early, but couldn't sleep.

A few minutes after ten o'clock he heard his parents come home. His mother went straight to David's room. She had a kind of "different" look on her face.

"David," she began. She hesitated, and then went on. "You know, dear, we want you to feel free to ask any questions about your birth parents . . ." She fumbled a bit and looked uncertain. "Have we answered all the questions you have? Is there anything more you want to know?"

David shrugged his shoulders, trying to look indifferent.

Then his dad came in. His look was tender as he told David, "Get to sleep, son. You don't want to be groggy at school tomorrow."

Somehow David felt better, knowing that his parents recognized that he was "different" and that he might be feeling pain because of it.

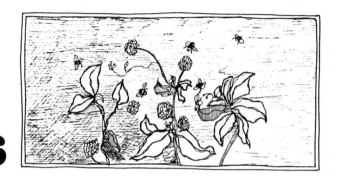

6

At the beginning of his first year in high school, David felt friendless, except for Diana. But Diana was a girl. A guy ought to have other guys for friends. David had been avoiding Alex Parsons ever since Diana had told him about Alex's going around saying that the reason for David's being so weird was that he was adopted.

Jimmy, who had lived next door to David when they were both little, had moved to another house after his twin sisters were born. They had hardly seen each other since. But now he and David were not only in school together, but were in history class at the same hour.

"How about coming over to my house this Saturday?" David asked Jimmy one day after the class.

"Can't," Jimmy answered. "Steve Wilson and I are getting together on Saturday."

Feeling rebuffed and hurt, there flashed through David's mind the picture of Jimmy at age five, taunting him with having "two mothers."

Afterward, he saw Jimmy, Steve, and a couple of others whispering in a group. Occasionally a voice rose above the whispering.

Once David thought he heard, "Oh, no! That's why . . ."

They're talking about me, David thought.

It seemed to David that everyone avoided him. Or was he avoiding them? Every time he passed a group they looked at him strangely, he thought. He felt terrible—sad and alone.

David brooded more and more about his being adopted. He fantasized that his REAL parents were losers. He raged inwardly, thinking of himself as awkward, stupid and bad. Had his real parents even *tried* to control themselves? Were they sex maniacs? Were they on drugs when they *made* him? He hated them!

He began to have sexual fantasies himself. He wondered if he should smoke some pot and get high enough to try something with Diana. It made him excited and gooey inside just to think about "doing it" with her. But would she? Or would he lose her friendship? Might it be better to try it first with someone who was already into sex? But even then, would he have the courage? Maybe if he could first get high on something . . .

Jim Stebbins and Scott Grainger were known to be drug pushers and had approached David once or twice, but had given up on him. It might be fun to get friendly with them, David thought, and become part of that clique.

One day he decided to approach Scott, but lost his nerve. Instead, he went home and talked roughly to his mother. At dinner that evening he sat silent and sulky. He wanted to hurt his parents. After a few attempts on their part to get into conversation with him, they gave up and talked to each other. That hurt even more, but there was a certain pleasure in feeling his pain. He wanted to hurt himself as much as he wanted to hurt them.

He felt guilty about having sexual thoughts about Diana. *Am I a sex maniac?* he asked himself. He decided to avoid her. The thought of losing her friendship saddened him, but it was better than taking the chance of her guessing what was on his mind.

24

The next day he left for school earlier than usual, so that he would miss meeting her. As he passed her house he felt that he no longer had even a single friend.

Later, as David was going into his French class, Diana stopped him. "David, what happened to you this morning? I waited and waited, and then I phoned your house. Your mother said you left early. She didn't know why. Why didn't you call me?"

David shrugged his shoulders.

"You haven't been very friendly lately. Is something wrong?"

How could he admit to Diana what he had been thinking about? "Naw," he answered carelessly.

"Something's wrong, David. I know it. I feel it. Can't you tell me, please?"

If he told her the truth he might lose her friendship forever, he thought. Hoping he sounded kind of careless and not really hurt, he said, "None of the guys like me. They talk about me, and when I get close they stop talking and look at me funny. I think it's because I'm adopted."

"That's silly, David. I think you're just imagining things. *I* like you. You know that, don't you?"

"I suppose."

"I guess you'd like to have more friends, wouldn't you? But David, you act like you don't *want* any friends. *I* know you want them, but *they* don't."

David remained silent. She just doesn't understand, he thought.

The next morning Diana was halfway to his house before they met.

"Just didn't want you to pass me up again," she teased.

They talked about other things, but David sensed that Diana was sure that he could be friends with the other boys if he tried. He felt good about her wanting to walk to school with him every day, and they resumed their usual comfortable talks. David pushed aside his longing to touch her, to hold her. He kept his feelings far back in his mind when he saw her.

Only at night, as he began to fall asleep, did he allow himself to think of her, to imagine himself holding her in his arms, touching her, being touched and fondled. Often he quickly made his bed in the morning to cover up the telltale indications of his sexual arousal.

David especially enjoyed art class. It was almost the only bright spot in his life right now. After the day that he had astonished his mother by observing that the abstract painting on which she was working had the shape of a mother and baby, his mother had arranged a "studio" for him in the laundry room and more than ever encouraged him to develop his artistic bent. "I've known for a long time that you have talent, David," she told him. "Perhaps it's in your genes. Mrs. Nelson told us that one of the reasons we were chosen to be your parents was because there was artistic talent in your birth family."

One day in art class, absorbed in painting a watercolor, he became aware of a commotion behind him. He looked up to find practically the whole class surrounding him.

Someone had noticed what he was painting and had called the others over to take a look. Jimmy, Steve Wilson, Sean Allen, Alex Parsons, and Buzz Cramer were all in the picture.

"Hey, that's my baseball cap, and it's on ME!" Buzz yelled. "He's painted me with my baseball cap on, just the way I wear it!"

"And that's my sweater," George Allen shouted. "Look, he's got the colors and the pattern just right!"

Jimmy said, "That's me and my UCLA T-shirt!"

"That's my baseball bat! Look, he's even got my name on it, just the way I printed it! And those are my jeans!"

David felt a wonderful glow, all the more thrilling because he wasn't expecting such interest and appreciation.

They like it, they like it! he marveled.

The class crowded around him. With all the attention they were giving him, David thought that maybe he didn't have to always feel alone and sorry for himself.

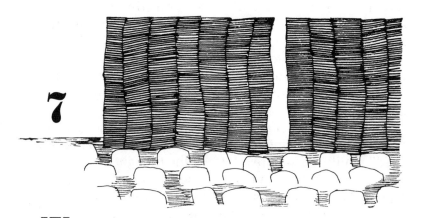

7

There was a boy at school to whom David felt drawn. His name was Jason Cummings. Nobody had a good word to say about Jason. Diana especially disliked him. David had often seen him with Jim Stebbins and Scott Grainger, so it didn't surprise David when Diana told him that Jason smoked pot. Also, that he had gotten Claire "in trouble."

"What do you mean, Diana? Did he talk her into smoking pot?"

"Worse than that. He got her started off on sex. Now they go out a lot together. There's even some talk about her having had an abortion."

Diana's gossip excited David. Jason fascinated him—the way Jason looked at girls . . . the way they looked back!

David wondered if he had been born because some-one like Jason had got someone like Claire "in trouble." It was not his favorite fantasy. He liked to think of himself as having been born to two persons who were in love but

27

couldn't marry. Or maybe the guy went off to war or got killed in an accident. Or the mother died in childbirth and there were no relatives.

David hoped he hadn't been born to rough kids like Jason and Claire. His mother was always pointing out to David, especially when he was misbehaving, "Think ahead! You can't just act on impulse." His mother really bored David when she talked like that. Sometimes he answered angrily, "Aw, Mom, what do you take me for? An idiot? I don't need any sermons! I can take care of myself."

David could take his father's "man-to-man" talks better. Dad always told David the facts of life straight on. Alcohol, drugs—a guy had to be careful not to get into bad habits.

David's worst moments were when he thought of the possibility that he might have come from "bad" parents or a "bad" family. He was revolted by the thought.

Or that there might be something "bad" in him. Maybe, he reasoned, there is some "badness" in all of us. Maybe the things that Jason was doing excited David because he was getting some of the thrill of being "bad" without the blame that would fall on him if he did all those "awful" things himself!

He mentioned this theory to Diana, and she laughed as she looked at him fondly. "Oh, David, what an idea! Who but someone like you would ever have thought of something like that? You're becoming a regular shrink!"

The way Diana looked at him with affection sent that "gooey" feeling through him again. But it quickly left as he began to think about how he could "test his theory." (That was the way his parents would have put it—"test his theory.")

He started to hang around Jason and made some friendly overtures to him. Jason began to notice David, and one day offered him a puff of the cigarette he was smoking.

"No, thanks," David said, "but tell me, what does it make you feel like?"

David knew that it was grass that Jason was smoking. David's parents disapproved of marijuana. Besides, it was illegal. But Jason's bravado, his ability to carry it off boldly, with no effort to hide what he was doing, gave David a kind of thrill. It was almost as if he were doing it himself.

"It makes me feel great!" Jason told him. "Why don't you try it? Just once, come on!" David shook his head and Jason looked disgusted. "Bullshit! You lightweight!" he sneered.

"I just don't feel like it," David said. "I was sick to my stomach this morning."

Jason puffed hard and a dreamy smile spread over his face. "Hey," he said, "how would you like to go to a skin flick? I know how to get in."

"OK," David said. He could feel himself taking on a rough, careless manner. School had let out for the day. He was expected home, but he thought to himself, "So what? It's time Mom got used to the idea that I don't have to get home on the dot, like some brainwashed kid."

They went to the movie. Jason had a way of sneaking in up a fire escape and through a back door. The door was locked, but Jason opened it with a knife, and David found himself in the balcony of the movie house.

They huddled there, watching. It was mostly a puzzle to David, but he got something of a thrill seeing all the pretty girls with their large breasts. The men were naked, too, and David saw what he supposed Mom and Dad did after they went to bed. They made sounds like those David heard coming out of Dad's and Mom's bedroom one night when he suspected they had been making love.

It was dark when Jason and David got out of the movie. Mom will worry and I'm sure to catch hell, David thought.

"Want to come home for dinner?" he asked. (It would be easier to face his parents if Jason were with him.)

"Sure," Jason said.

"Don't you have to let your parents know first?"

"No, neither of them are home, anyhow. It's Dad's poker night. Mom's at work."

"This late?"

"Yeah, she doesn't go to work till five o'clock."

Jason was opening up a new world to David. He didn't know many kids whose parents left them alone at night a lot.

David felt uncomfortable as they neared his house. He realized that his mother had been watching from the window because she had the door open as they reached it.

"Thank goodness you're home," she said. "It isn't like you to be late. What happened?"

"This is Jason Cummings," David said, ignoring his mother's question.

She looked at Jason sharply.

"I invited Jason over for dinner. His folks aren't home."

"I'm glad to have you, Jason. Any friend of David's is welcome in our home."

It sounded to David like his mother really meant it. Her voice was cheery and her smile welcoming. But because of the way she was looking Jason up and down, David sensed that she wasn't getting a good impression.

Jason didn't come off too well at dinner, either. He didn't seem comfortable, even though David thought his parents were warm and pleasant, as they always were toward any guest in their home. Maybe he himself wasn't comfortable. David was embarrassed, for instance, at the bravado with which Jason pulled out and lit a cigarette while David helped his mother bring in dessert. He asked to be excused to show Jason his room.

At nine o'clock David's father came into the room. "Does Jason need a ride home?" he asked. "It's getting late."

"It's OK, Mr. Brooks. I can get home by myself. I don't mind being out late."

"I'd rather drive you home, if you don't mind."

Later, while David strained to hear, snatches of talk came to him from his parents' room. They sounded unhappy.

30

"Give him his freedom to choose . . . . He's a good kid!"

There was an answering murmur, then "He'll tire of this kind of friend . . . just an adventure . . . a taste of another world . . ."

But being with Jason made David feel part of the crowd. At least for the time being it made him feel important. All the kids at school wondered why the two of them were spending time together and meeting after school.

During the four weeks that his parents were attending the meetings at the Children's Bureau, David kept wishing that they would tell him more about what was going on. But somehow he didn't feel like asking.

It seemed to him that his mother was not as upset about his behavior as before. She seemed even more sure of herself. And although his father at times seemed to be trying to get closer to him, he was still as busy, if not more so, than usual. The result was that any "man-to-man" talks with his dad seemed to fizzle out pretty fast.

At last the four meetings for the parents at the Children's Bureau were over, and David and his parents were on the way to the first of the meetings for the teenagers. It was a ten-minute drive from their home, but David's eagerness to get there made it seem longer.

David was surprised as they approached the Children's Service Bureau. He had expected it to be an office building or an old remodeled house.

His mother said, "This is it!" They drove past a concrete block fence enclosing unkempt grounds. There was an opening in the fence. On one side a metal plaque read: CHILDREN'S SERVICE BUREAU. The plaque on the other side read: HILLCREST SCHOOL.

They turned into a road leading to the main building. A sign read:

CHILDREN

DRIVE CAREFULLY

They passed a cluster of small buildings. Children were playing outside. Some were roller-skating on a concrete mall that connected the buildings. Two boys were tossing a ball between them. Others—girls as well as boys—were gathered in small groups, talking or staring at the Brooks family as their car drove by.

His father was driving and his mother was sitting next to him in the front of the car. She turned around to look at David. Even with her back turned she seemed to have some kind of built-in antenna that always picked up his feelings, David thought.

"Are you finding this different from what you expected?" she asked.

"I sure am!" He could not keep the sound of panic from his voice. "Who are all these kids? Is this where I'd be living if you hadn't adopted me?"

"Heavens, no! If it hadn't been Dad and I who adopted you, you would have been grabbed up by one of at least twenty families who were waiting for a great son like you!"

"Who are they? Why are they here?"

His dad answered. "These are emotionally disturbed children."

"What does that mean?"

"Anything from being unhappy and . . . mopey—to, oh, making all kinds of trouble."

"Is it like a prison or a reform school?"

"Oh, no! They're here voluntarily."

"Were any of them adopted, and it didn't work out?"

David's mother answered, "Yes, dear, I understand that sometimes happens. But here we are!"

As David's father parked the car, David's mother gave her son a reassuring hug.

"Don't worry, David." She spoke in a firm voice. "You'll never need to live here. Your father and I guarantee you that."

The three of them walked toward a small house that bore a sign:

COMMUNITY SERVICES

David's first impression as they entered the large room where the parents and children were gathering was of a happy, talkative group. He found himself responding a bit shyly as his parents introduced him to some of the other parents, who in turn introduced David and his parents to the children with them.

He wanted to move around the room, to look at everyone and everything, but he hesitated. Then his eyes fell upon the person in the snapshot taken the day his parents had brought him home from the agency. Mrs. Nelson! Even fifteen years after it was taken, David recognized her from her picture. She approached him.

"I've been hearing about you from your parents, David. They are so proud of you!"

"I like them, too." They both laughed.

Mrs. Nelson introduced David to Mr. Perkins. He had a kind, smiling face. David liked him right away.

More parents and children came in. More introductions were made. It was confusing, meeting everyone all at once. It wasn't that there were so many, but everyone was talking. David didn't know where to look first. He felt drawn to some of the other kids, but somehow they held off from each other.

Did other parents love their children the way his parents loved him? Or were some of them sorry they had adopted? David wondered.

Finally, the children were led to the second floor, where they were to meet with Mr. Perkins, apart from the parents.

The parents were to meet with Mrs. Nelson.

9

Mr. Perkins and the group of young people entered a room with a large round table in the center that was surrounded by ten chairs. On the table in front of each chair was a card with a first name on it, written with a dark pen in large capital letters. Only one card had the whole name on it: RICHARD PERKINS.

A platter of cookies was on the table. A couple of kids grabbed two or three and began to eat.

There was some fooling around, especially by an older boy whose card read RICK. Rick was sitting across from a talkative girl named RACHEL. She was looking at Rick in a flirty way. Rick came around the table and tried to shove the boy sitting next to Rachel out of his seat.

34

"Rick, get back to your seat at once!" Mr. Perkins's voice was firm, but only loud enough to make himself clearly heard and to give the group the message that he meant business.

"Aw, Mr. Perkins, do we have to sit in a special place? Can't I sit next to Rachel?"

"Rick, where you sit is of no special concern, but it is disturbing to change places once we are seated. We're here for a purpose. Let's get on with it!"

Mr. Perkins paused, and when he began to speak again his voice changed from authoritative to gentle. The group had come together on matters that were important to each person, he said. Even Rick appeared to agree that it would be best to cooperate, at least for the time being.

"Why are we here?" Mr. Perkins asked. "Let's go around the table and give each one a chance to tell why you are here and what you hope to get out of these meetings." He turned to a morose-looking boy who was sitting on his left.

"Let's start with you, Adam."

"Well . . ." Adam began, looking as if he were really trying hard to think. "Uh . . . Mom asked us to come—me and my brother Chris here—because we're both adopted." He paused, looking a bit uncertain. Then words rushed out. He looked angry.

"We would like to find our father. Our parents were divorced when I was two years old and Chris was nine months old. My mother just went off and left us with our father. He tried to keep us for a while, but it was just too much for him. He played guitar in a rock group and had to be traveling a lot. So he put us in a foster home, and I guess that wasn't any good, either. Then he came here—to this place—and he signed us away." Adam brought his fists down on the table with an angry thud.

Chris, sitting next to Adam, took up the story.

"I don't care so much about looking for my father. I have a father—and a mother, too—and they're nice. I mean I like living with them. But I keep thinking about that other mother, why she left us. After all, when people fight and get

35

divorced, the mother usually takes care of the kids. What was wrong with us? Why did she do a thing like that—just walk out on us?"

David could hardly wait for Mr. Perkins's answer. Chris was saying things that exactly expressed some of David's feelings.

Mr. Perkins said, "We'll get back to you, Adam, and Chris. Right now we'll keep going around the table. Rick?"

"Yeah, well . . ." Rick began. He had been eyeing Rachel while Adam and Chris were talking. He hadn't even seemed to be listening, but now his shoulders tensed up and he began to talk fast in an angry tone of voice.

"I just want to find that woman who gave me away. I want to see what she looks like. I'm going to look her straight in the eye and tell her what a rotten thing that was for her to do!"

"Yes, we'll be talking some more about that," Mr. Perkins said. "Beth?"

Beth blushed. She looked shy, uncomfortable, afraid to talk.

Rick spoke up. "She's my kid sister, and she's thirteen. She never talks much. My mother does most of the talking for her."

Rick seemed ready to go on talking, but Mr. Perkins interrupted. "I'm sure she's capable of speaking for herself, Rick. Let's give her a chance." Mr. Perkins smiled and looked encouragingly toward Beth.

"I'm here because my mom and dad wanted me to come." Beth blushed a deep red. She looked as if she were going to cry.

Boy, she's pretty, David thought.

Mr. Perkins looked at her sympathetically.

Beth looked embarrassed but happy. She remained silent.

Philip was next. "I guess all of us are here because our parents wanted us to come. THEY are the ones who are having problems, not US! My father died two years ago, and my mother just sits around crying and feeling sorry for herself. She loves my brother, who was born two years after they adopted me. If they'd known they were going to have a baby themselves, they wouldn't have adopted ME!"

"It must be very hard for you to feel that way, Philip," Mr. Perkins said. "You'll get a chance to talk some more, and all of us will try to understand your feelings and help you with them."

David looked hard at Philip. He noticed how dark Philip was. His hair was black and slick. His nose was broad. He had very dark eyes, almost black. And they had a different shape from any other eyes he had seen before—except maybe in the movies. That was it! Philip looked almost as if he might be Indian—a native American—well, not quite, but almost.

Ellen was next. "I didn't want to come at all," she said. "What's the use? I'm adopted, and nothing can change that. My parents made me come."

Mr. Perkins looked sympathetic. David felt a little sorry for Ellen. Something made him feel a little sorry for himself, too.

Ellen was an attractive girl, even though she was a little fat, David thought. Well, not really fat, just plump. Her words were angry, but her voice was not. Hurt, perhaps, sad, disappointed. But not really angry.

"Rachel?"

Rachel shrugged. She looked the group over with that sexy look she'd been throwing Rick's way ever since they had first come into the room. But the sexy look faded as she began to speak.

"I want to find my mother. My parents adopted me because they had two boys and they wanted a girl. But they didn't want anyone like me, that's for sure. My brothers are smart—studying and doing all the right things. But me? I can't please them, anyhow, so I'd just as soon have some fun!" Rachel tossed her head, and her long, thick auburn hair bounced around a bit as she gave Rick one of those flirty looks again.

"We'll talk some more about that," Mr. Perkins said.

David wondered when Mr. Perkins was going to get down to business. When will he tell us some of the things we want to know? How do we find out why we were signed away? How can we find our birth parents, talk to them, maybe see them? David began to feel impatient.

"Carl, tell us about you," Mr. Perkins was saying.

David found himself intrigued that such a little boy— he couldn't be more than eleven years old—had come into this group of teenagers. Why?

Carl had been fidgeting a lot while the others were talking. His chair had been making creaky sounds. As he began to speak in his childlike voice, David felt a kind of protectiveness toward him.

"My mom and dad made me come because they say I'm bad! The school is always sending notes home because I don't pay attention." He paused and took a deep breath. His voice was angry as he continued.

"Everyone's mad at me because I fight with the other kids. But it's their fault, not mine. The guys keep teasing me about my real parents not wanting me, but I'm not going to let them pick on me. I want a drink of water. Can I go out and get a drink?"

"In just a minute, Carl. We're almost finished going around the table. I'd like you to stay and hear David."

David was the last one to be called on. "I'm here," he began, his voice firm and controlled despite the inner agitation he was feeling, "because I wanted to come. I was wishing I could meet other kids who were adopted. I don't like being the only one in my class who's adopted—at least I think I'm the only one in my class who's adopted, maybe the only one in my school."

David paused. Could he really tell all the thoughts and feelings that were locked up inside of him?

Mr. Perkins was looking at him so kindly that David decided he could trust him. Words came tumbling out.

"I want to know all about those people who gave me away. My parents keep telling me they'll answer any questions I have, but I don't like to ask them. I have a weird dream that scares me. I think it has something to do with my being adopted."

Rick said, "I'd like to hear that one."

"All right," Mr. Perkins said. "If David would like to tell us about it, I think we all might like to hear it. He's the last one to be called on, so he can be the first to tell us more."

"At first I didn't know it was a dream," David began. "It seemed so real."

Carl must have forgotten he wanted a drink. He sat so still you would think he was glued to his chair. Even Rick was looking at David bug-eyed. Rachel stopped batting her eyes at Rick. Ellen looked straight at David, momentarily forgetting her sadness. So were the others—Adam, Chris, Philip . . . and Beth!

10

"**I** felt wide awake," David began, unaware of everyone in the room as he relived his dream. Eyes glazed, terror in his voice, he came to the climax of his nightmare.

"The sound of footsteps comes, creeping up the stairs. The door opens and a person wearing a mask comes into my room, throws a blanket over my head, grabs me, and creeps down the stairs, holding me as I scream and kick.

39

Then I wake up, yelling 'HELP! HELP!' "

Still shaking and sweating, David heard Mr. Perkins's voice, saying, "Dreams are often hard to understand, David. Sometimes they are thoughts or feelings that have been buried deep because they are too painful or frightening to face. When we are beginning to be ready to deal with what's bothering us, it shows up in our dreams." He paused. "How do you feel about being adopted, David?"

"Oh, I'm happy, I guess. But I wish . . . I wish I knew who those other people were, the ones who 'made' me. Sometimes I'm angry because they shouldn't have had me if they couldn't keep me."

"You would like to unmask the figure in your dreams," Mr. Perkins said gently.

"Oh, yes! I'm sure it isn't my mom or dad. I know they didn't steal me. They got me here at this agency."

Carl began to stutter, "y-y-y-y-You know what I think? I think David's mad at the lady who gave him away. I mean the lady who 'borned' him. He loves his mom and dad and he doesn't want the lady who 'borned' him to take him back. He doesn't know whether the person in the mask is a man or a woman, but whoever it is, he makes that masked person steal him. That way he can stop being mad at the lady—or the man—who 'borned' him, because he knows that at least one of them wants him back. He can't be mad at his mom and dad because he *knows* they didn't steal him. So where does it get him, to have a dream like that?"

David laughed, along with the others in the group. Carl looked around the room, grinning broadly.

Mr. Perkins said, "I guess we'd better call you 'Mr. Freud,' Carl."

Everyone laughed again.

No question, David thought, he's smart for his age. No wonder they let him in with us older kids.

Rachel looked as if she would like to hug him, as she said, "You're cute, Carl." She gave him a knowing look and added, "I bet I know where you learned stuff like that."

I wonder what she means, David thought. Could it

possibly have something to do with seeing a shrink?

Mr. Perkins paused, and when he spoke, it was in a gentle, kind manner, like a doctor explaining a mild sickness. "Sometimes we are unable to express our anger toward persons we love. So our anger goes underground and comes out in our dreams, disguised so that we won't feel guilty about it." Then Mr. Perkins continued in his usual calm manner.

"Well, now," he said, "it seems that most of you want to know about your birth parents. Some of you want to find them. Probably all of you would like to see what they look like. And some of you may wish that you could talk with them. Some of you feel angry with them for having given you up."

"Yeah, that's right," several voices murmured. Heads nodded in agreement.

"I want you to know that I am not here to help you find them, or to tell you how you can find them on your own. But it's important for you to talk about what you are feeling about them. And if you are angry, let's get it out in the open."

Mr. Perkins paused, and another murmur spread throughout the room. Rick was heard to say, "Yeah, man!" Philip turned as red as his dark skin allowed. His eyes looked popping mad, as if they were ready to come out of his head.

"But first let's get our terms straight," Mr. Perkins continued. "When we are talking about the REAL parents, whom do we mean?"

Adam said, "Those are the parents who gave birth to you."

Several voices agreed.

David said, "I don't think they are the REAL parents. My parents have taken care of me since I was eight days old. I depend on them for everything. Food, clothes, a place to live, an allowance—all that stuff."

David paused. "Go on, David," Mr. Perkins said. "We're listening."

"And they care about what happens to us, don't they? If your birth parents keep you and do all those things, then of course *they* are the REAL parents."

David hoped he didn't sound like a show-off. Rick was looking at him with a sneer. David wished that he could sink through the floor.

But Mr. Perkins nodded in approval, and Beth and Chris looked as if they agreed.

Rachel spoke up. "Mom calls her 'the other lady.' But *she* was the one who had me in her body. She was the one whose ovum got fertilized by a sperm. She kept me in her until the fertilized egg became a real baby, ready to come out into the world. I would call her the birth mother."

"Birth mother—that's a good way to describe her," Mr. Perkins said. "And what about the father?"

Rick spoke up in a loud, contemptuous voice. "Aw, he didn't do anything but have a good time."

"How many of you feel that way?" Mr. Perkins asked.

The group sat silent. Rick looked as if he realized that maybe he had gone too far. David was startled. He had never really believed that his birth father was someone just having a good time, and he sensed that others in the group felt the same way, or *wanted* to feel the same way.

"A great many people think that the father doesn't care," Mr. Perkins said. "But I have met many birth fathers who came in with the mother to plan for the baby. Many of them were young people whom I liked and respected."

"They just didn't think ahead," David mumbled. His face reddened. He felt embarrassed when he thought of himself as being what guys like Rick called "weird."

All the same, David felt pleased with himself when Mr. Perkins answered, "That's right, David, they didn't think ahead. What would you do if you found yourself in such a position?"

Carl didn't wait for David to answer. He burst out loudly, "I wouldn't get in that position. I want to finish college and get a good job and get married before I have a baby."

42

Rick said, "My birth parents were married. They had all the children they wanted. Their business was going down the tubes and they couldn't handle another expense when I was born."

"Rick, perhaps your case is different from most. But you have something in common with everyone else in this room."

"Yeah, none of our parents kept us," said Ellen in a sad voice.

"What are some of the reasons why birth parents can't keep a child born to them?"

A lively discussion broke out. It seemed that most of the group knew that their birth parents were young, still in school, and not ready to settle down, raise a family and make a living for them, as the parents who had adopted them could do.

Ellen sat silent during this discussion. Now she raised her hand and waved it until Mr. Perkins noticed and called on her.

"Some people just don't like children," she said sadly. "I know a family like that. I baby-sit for them."

"Yes, that happens sometimes, and it is very sad. The problem for each of you is different, isn't it? As you understand it, your birth parents were not in a position to give you the care that children need. How come?"

Rick blurted out, "It's because they're normal. Everybody gets those feelings. They want to make love. I've done it, and it's great! Are we supposed to go into a monastery or something?" Rick gave Rachel a long look and squirmed in his chair.

Mr. Perkins then led the group into a discussion of how to handle sexual feelings. He didn't lecture them on morality, David noticed. He wasn't recommending cold showers and jogging. He just hit them cold with their responsibility to prevent pregnancies. From there the group went on to discuss contraceptives.

Rachel spoke up. "Suppose you fell in love and couldn't marry, or knew that marriage wouldn't work out. I know what I'd do. I'd get a diaphragm. And if I accidentally got pregnant, I'd have an abortion. And if it was too late to have an abortion, I would have the baby and go on welfare. I wouldn't want my baby to feel the way I do, that the mother who gave birth to me didn't want me and gave me away."

Almost everyone agreed, or seemed to. Heads nodded. Looks of sympathy were expressed on some faces. But David was uneasy. His face reddened again, and he wanted to speak, but no words came out.

"David?" Mr. Perkins asked.

"Well, I know a girl who has a baby and feeds it beer and neglects it. If it weren't that she lives with her parents, I don't know how that baby would stay alive and grow up to be normal. I wouldn't want to be her baby any more than I would want to have parents who didn't like children."

Carl added, "Yeah, and the papers are full of stories about babies left at supermarkets and of kids beaten up by their parents. How would you like to be one of those babies?"

Philip burst out in anger. "OK! So maybe it was better to be adopted than to stay with someone too young to take care of you, or too selfish to have children, or so angry with the world and everyone in it that they took it out on their kids. But who says the people who adopt you are going to be great parents? How do you know?"

"That's a good question, Philip," Mr. Perkins said. "We do the best we can to make sure. Most of the couples who come to our agency to adopt have a strong desire for a child. They have to answer a great many questions that make them think about why they really want a child. We want to know why they want to be a family. We try to make sure in every way we can that they know something about what it's like to take care of children—not just when they are cute, cuddly little babies, but while they are growing up. We not only try to understand why they want a child, but we also try to make sure, insofar as it is possible to evaluate these qualities, that they have the capacity to be *good* parents."

"But think of this," Mr. Perkins finished in a firm, no-

44

nonsense tone of voice, "we have to go on from where we are. You are adopted, and that is that! Let's see what it means to you."

Ellen spoke up in a voice filled with sadness. "I'm adopted, and nothing can change that."

"But it doesn't have to get you down," Chris said.

And Rachel added, "Look, we're all in this together. We're not alone."

"Exactly," Mr. Perkins said. "That's why we're here."

David felt relieved to hear the others talk angrily about their birth parents, asking what right they had to give a baby away. Why did they have to have babies if they couldn't keep them?

As they left, the group seemed quieter, calmer.

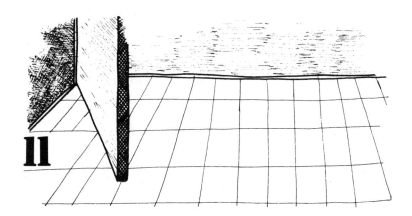

11

As he was getting into bed that night after the group meeting, David remembered something that had happened a long time ago. The memory came into his mind like a picture. How old could he have been—seven or eight, maybe younger?

He had gone into the bathroom that connected his room to his parents'. Their door had been slightly open. He had seen that the sky was no longer dark, so he had not needed to turn on the light. But it must have been quite early in the morning, for he felt the heaviness of unfinished sleep.

Unusual sounds were coming from his parents' bedroom. At that time he had believed they were sounds of pain. Low, breathless moans and little squeals. He now realized that what he had believed were the cries of someone being hurt had actually been sounds of pleasure.

Then he heard his father's voice, but couldn't make out what he was saying. The sound was muffled, as if he were face down on a pillow. But his mother's voice was clear, and it held a note of sadness that made him listen hard.

"Oh yes, Jon, I do mind! I feel bad—for you and for me. I wish I could even once have seen the face and held to my breast the little body of the child that I might have borne for you. All those years of waiting and wanting!"

"How do you feel now that you have David? Does it make you feel better even if . . ."

David had not heard the rest. His father's voice had come out clearly at first, then was muffled again.

"Oh, yes, Jon! I remember so well how sad it was to be childless. But those feelings are gone. I am a mother now. I love David. He has almost made me forget the old pain. I needed him so much. He has filled the emptiness, and I love him dearly. True, it cannot be the same as if I had given birth to him myself. Still, he is truly mine—no one else's." His mother's voice held a note of fierceness that David now sharply remembered.

A feeling of elation came over him as David said to himself, "Yes, they needed me, both of them. And I needed them!"

12

The next three meetings of the group passed quickly—too quickly for David. He liked being with others who had been adopted. That strange feeling of being "different" bothered him much less now that he knew others who were "different" in the same way that he was.

He hadn't realized how angry he felt about having been "given away" until he had heard some of the others expressing exactly the same kind of feelings. The terrifying nightmares he used to have still puzzled him, but the thought of them no longer frightened him.

David now understood that he had been angry about having been adopted. In some mysterious way that dreams express thoughts that a person cannot face head on, his anger toward his mom and dad for adopting him had gone underground. It had come out in his dreams, distorted, but releasing his conflicts and revealing his true joy and faith in his parents, especially his mother.

Although the riddle and conflict about being adopted had not been completely resolved, he was on his way toward understanding and accepting the fact of it, although he still needed to understand more about why it had been necessary.

There were changes taking place at home, too. David was getting along better with his parents. His mother didn't seem as upset about his behavior. And his father didn't seem to have his mind always on his work, nor did he excuse himself after dinner as early or as often as possible.

His parents listened with great interest to anything David told them about what was going on in his group. But they did not ask questions or tell him what was going on in their group.

However, they talked about themselves more often than they used to, of their feelings about being adoptive parents. David had not realized that they also felt "different." They, too, had been hurt by other people's reactions to David's being adopted.

"People actually apologize to you when you tell them that your child is adopted. The typical reaction is, "Oh, Mrs. Brooks, I'm so sorry! Please excuse me!"

The three of them laughed at the tone of voice she took on as she mimicked these remarks, and her husband, looking at her lovingly, said, "Laura, you are really something!"

"I guess what bothers me most," she continued, "is when someone gushes about my being 'noble' to have taken on 'someone else's child.' 'Noble!' I was getting the child I wanted with all my heart! And oh, David," she finished with a deep sigh, "you can't believe the joy you brought me when I held you in my arms."

David knew that his mother wished that she had given birth to him herself. He again vividly recalled the night he had overheard his parents without their knowing it. She had *needed* him! It made him feel good to know that whoever had "given him away" had done something good for *his* mother.

13

David felt a tinge of sadness as they drove to the last session. Would he ever see any of the group again? He would miss them. As they gathered in "their" room, and as he looked into each face, he realized how close to them he felt, how much more he understood them, and knew about them, than he did about his schoolmates.

Mr. Perkins allowed the group a few minutes to settle down. Then he asked, "Would any of you like to ask any questions, or clear up any thoughts you have about the things we've been talking about?"

"I have a question," Rick said. "Why isn't Philip here? I just saw him on the grounds as we drove up. He told me he was living here at Hillcrest. How come?"

Mr. Perkins hesitated, then answered slowly, "He wanted to come here. He wanted to be away from home for a while and get some help with his feelings."

"Is it OK to tell this gang here what he told me?" Rick persisted.

"Do you think he would want you to tell?"

"You bet. He told me. And he knew I was coming here. So why not? He didn't swear me to secrecy," Rick sneered.

It was easy to see that Mr. Perkins wasn't happy, but he had always said that the group was free to talk about anything they wanted to talk about, and asked that everyone listen to the one who needed to talk.

It was obvious that everyone wanted to hear what Rick had to say. David himself was bursting with curiosity. He had always wondered about Philip. Why was he so different-looking? Underneath all Philip's rough talk, too, there was something sad about him. They listened intently as Rick, relishing the eagerness with which the group waited for him to speak, began.

"Well, I got it straight from the horse's mouth. Philip told me his mother didn't want him. He said she told everyone he was part Indian and then she called THEM prejudiced. SHE was the one who was sorry she didn't have a nice blonde, blue-eyed little girl, like she wanted in the first place.

"Philip was so mad at his mother he wanted to get even with her for loving Tom and not loving him. She worked hard to make a living for the three of them. She manages a dress shop, and she always came home so tired she'd just flop into a chair and kick off her shoes.

"Philip said HE was the one who got dinner ready for the three of them when his mother came home all worn out. He had to push Tom into helping him. Sometimes he punched Tom, and then his mother would get angry and yell at Philip. He claimed she even beat him.

"I asked him what else he did to make her so mad at him. Believe me, I know all the things you can do to get 'even' when you're mad at someone. Philip wasn't going to tell all the things he did, but I got it out of him. I told him all the things I do to get even with my mom for the way she treats me.

"So then Philip admitted that he stole money from his mother's purse, didn't do his homework, argued with teachers, and fought with the kids at school and in the neighborhood.

"I didn't get all this right away. But when I showed him I knew a thing or two about these situations he couldn't

50

squirm out of it or act like an angel, the way he used to do here in this room.

"I guess it was when they went visiting and he set fire to something in the garage of his mother's best friend that she got fed up and got him admitted here at Hillcrest. Isn't that right, Mr. Perkins?"

Mr. Perkins looked sad and uncomfortable. Then he answered slowly, looking around at each of the faces turned toward him. The group waited eagerly for his response. Some looked almost afraid of what they were going to hear.

"When someone comes to this agency," he began, "or to this room where we are meeting as a group, whatever is said here is not repeated outside. It is a professional confidence." Mr. Perkins paused, and looked around at each face in the group. He wore a solemn, serious look. He seemed to be pleading for their understanding.

Rick looked a bit uncomfortable. But he shrugged his shoulders as if to say, "Who cares?" He was sitting next to Rachel. He looked as if he might be holding her hand under the table. David had a feeling that Rachel and Rick would be seeing a lot of each other after these sessions were over.

Ellen leaned forward. Her eyes glistened with unshed tears. She seemed about to say something, then shook her head and sat back in her chair. David wished that he could reach over and tell Ellen how much he liked her, how much he wanted her to say whatever it might be that she had on her mind.

Mr. Perkins said gently, "Ellen, tell us what you are thinking, please."

Ellen blushed. A little vein in her neck stuck out. Then words came out of her throat in a rush, in a flood of pent-up feelings. She took a Kleenex out of her pocket and twisted it in her hands as she talked.

"I feel sorry for Philip. I can understand what he is feeling. I feel unwanted, too—well, maybe unneeded is a better word. First of all, my birth parents rejected me." Her voice was shaking. She paused to wipe the tears that were running down her cheeks. A determined look came into her face. She shook herself, and when she spoke again her voice was firm and strong.

"My parents adopted me because they already had three boys and wanted a daughter. My mother didn't know that she was two months pregnant when they brought me home from the agency. When she realized it, she told the social worker, and the agency wanted to take me back.

"But Mom and Dad said they loved me, and they begged to keep me. Looking back now, I suppose even as little as I was, I must have missed Mom terribly when she went to the hospital to have the baby. Don't you think that even though I was only one year old I must have felt something?"

Ellen looked toward Mr. Perkins and he said, "Of course!"

"Then Mom gave birth to Julie, the daughter they had longed for! I can just imagine how excited and happy everyone must have been when Julie was born.

"I don't know how old I was when I began to be jealous of Julie. I must have felt *something*, with all that excitement going on. It seems like I've *always* been jealous of Julie. Even now, sometimes I just can't stand her!

"Then my parents decided—so they told me—that it would be better for me not to be the only one in the family who was adopted. So when Julie was two years old they adopted Donald. But what good did it do *me*? Mom couldn't handle it all, and Dad was busy with his work. And so then I was jealous of *both* Julie and Donald!

"I used to think that was the reason they sent Donald away. But my parents told me that they realized that something was wrong with Donald right from the beginning. Then they found out that he had all kinds of birth defects. The agency wanted to take Donald back, but my parents said no. Donald needed a home and they wanted to give him one, they said. But I thought Donald's trouble was my fault, because I was so jealous. Finally they had to put Donald in a special school for the deaf and retarded. I saw him last week

52

and I cried! He's so beautiful! But to be deaf *and* retarded—how terrible for him!"

Ellen's voice broke and she began to cry.

Quick as a flash, Rachel was beside her, hugging her close. It was easy to see that Rachel was full of love, and that it wasn't just the sexy kind.

Ellen dried her eyes. Clinging to Rachel's hand, she said, "There's something else I'd like to tell you. When I learned how babies were made, I was furious with my father. I don't think it was just because I was jealous of Julie. Or that I felt cheated because there were so many of us. I suppose that may have been part of it. But he should have been more considerate of my mom. She had too much to do. She was always tired. DAD was never tired!

"Do you know that I didn't talk to my father for months before we came here? I didn't want to come at all. I hated even driving here with my dad. I used to get away from home as much as I could when I knew he was going to be there.

"After I'd come here a couple of times, I began to talk with my dad for the first time in, I don't know how long. He told me how much he loved me, and how sorry he was about having a baby so soon after adopting me. They hadn't known Mom was pregnant, and they had wanted a baby so much.

"I know now that my father is a good person. I'm sorry I used to hurt him by not talking to him." Ellen began to cry. David was thinking what a change this was for a girl who had felt so hopeless when the group first met.

Everyone was quiet. Then, even before Mr. Perkins could clear his throat and start to say something, Rachel—still standing beside Ellen—said, "Ellen, I wish I had a sister like you. I hope we can see each other from now on and be friends."

Ellen looked up at Rachel. Her smile was beautiful as they hugged each other.

David watched Rachel as she returned to her seat beside Rick. She had seemed like a different person when she was comforting Ellen. But there she was, swinging her hips again as she walked toward her seat. And as she sat down beside Rick she gave him a long look. David noticed that Rick's right hand and Rachel's left went right back under the table again!

It was Beth's turn to say something. She just sat there, blushing. Mr. Perkins said, "We'd like to hear from you, Beth. Tell us how you feel about being adopted, or anything else you'd like to say. You know that in this group you may say anything you like."

But Beth just sat there, blushing. David felt sorry for her.

Then came the sound of voices signaling that the parents were outside the door and the session was over. Everyone seemed relieved that Beth—so painfully shy and unsure of herself—wouldn't have to talk.

Some day, David said to himself, some day I'll get her to talk to me.

14

David's summer vacation had begun, and he was just getting up one morning when the phone rang.

"It's for you, David," his mother called out.

It was Rick. "Hiya, Davey old boy, whatcha doing this afternoon?"

"What did you have in mind, Rick?"

"I've got lots to tell you. I'd like to come over and visit you. My dad's moving his business to South Carolina. He's bought a house there already, and we're all moving in a couple of weeks, as soon as we can get packed."

His mother was surprised to learn that Rick was coming over.

"I'm surprised, too, Mom."

"Why, David?"

"Well, for one thing, he's much older than I. He's seventeen, maybe eighteen by now. And besides, we're so different."

"How, David?"

"Well, Rick was always fooling around in our group and flirting with Rachel. When our group first began, he threw spitballs until Mr. Perkins stopped him. Did his parents say anything about him in the meetings of your group?"

David noticed that his mother hesitated before she spoke.

"Well, I suppose you know that the family moved here because Rick was found to have 'learning disabilities.' They chose to live here because Rick's mother had made a special study of the schools all over the country. The one she wanted for Rick was out here in California."

"Yes, Rick said something like that—he told us about his learning difficulties and said that his mother was 'an expert at diagnosis.' That was the way he put it—kind of sarcastically. I'm really interested in finding out more about Rick, Mom. It sounds like he wants to tell me something. It might help me to know more about what you know about him, don't you think so?"

Mrs. Brooks hesitated, then said slowly, choosing her words carefully. "Rick's mother was having a pretty hard time with him. He was so disruptive at his friends' parties that he wasn't being invited to people's homes any more. What was he like in your group, David?"

"I told you. He did a lot of messing around—is that what you mean by being disruptive?"

She nodded. She looked as if she could say a great

deal more. David thought it best not to push at this point, although he hoped that some day he would get the whole story.

Rick arrived after lunch, insisting that he had already eaten. David's mother served some milk and cookies. They went outdoors to lounge on the grass in the sunshine, lying on their stomachs and facing each other. David relaxed, happy to see Rick, wondering what was to come. Clearly, Rick had something on his mind, and at last he came out with it.

"You know, David, you were the only halfway normal kid in our group. That's why I want to tell you about something that happened to me. I have to tell *someone* and I can't tell my parents. They'd be awful mad at me if they knew."

David nodded. He knew exactly what Rick meant.

"Well, I was eighteen just before school was over, and I decided that just as soon as school let out I'd run away. I wanted to find the woman who gave me up."

David recalled how angry Rick had been when he talked about "that woman who gave me away." He had said, "I'm going to look her straight in the eye and tell her what a rotten thing that was to do."

"I had some money saved up—I knew I had to have some money. Also, on my birthday I got a big check from my parents and another from my Grandma. So I just took everything I had in my bank account and I split. I left my folks a note, so they wouldn't go looking for me or reporting me to the Missing Persons Bureau, or anything like that.

"After all, I was eighteen. I had my driver's license, so that was going to help—even though my folks thought I was too irresponsible to have a car of my own, or even to use theirs very much.

"I went to New York. There's an organization there that was formed by an adopted woman who wrote a book about her own trouble finding her birth mother.

"Oh, yeah, I forgot to mention that I had my birth certificate with me. I found out that the town I was born in

56

was in a state where if you had your amended birth certificate, the one showing the date you were born, the hospital and the city—and if you could prove you were the person you said you were, and if you were over eighteen— you could look at your original birth certificate! I lit out of there so fast I forgot to ask where I could get a bus to take me to the town I was looking for.

"It took a little doing, but by that time I was used to finding my way around. I got there, all right. I found the City Hall and got the information on the original birth certificate. Then I got on the phone. The information operator gave me the phone numbers of everyone in the area who had the last name on my original birth certificate.

"I called three numbers before I found the right one. Some woman answered the phone, and when I asked her if she knew anyone by the name of Anthony Swenson, born eighteen years ago on May 15, she started to cry.

"I told her that's who I was, and that I would like to see her."

David waited in suspense for the rest of the story.

"Was I surprised! She was a sick, tired old woman. She must have had me when she was about forty years old! By that time she already had four children, all boys. When I was born, she and her husband—it's not easy to call him my father, or even my birth father—were running a grocery store. It was one of those Mom-and-Pop stores, and the chain stores were giving them stiff competition. The husband was in poor health.

"The old woman told me they didn't see how they could take care of another child. The doctor told them he knew a fine family in New York who wanted a child. They were 'wonderful people,' he said. They could give this child a good home and would pay all medical and hospital bills. In appreciation, they would give each boy in the family a United States Treasury Bond. Turns out they cashed the bonds that same year in order to pay the funeral expenses when the old man died.

"The old lady ran the store by herself until her health gave out and she didn't have the strength to keep on. Her sons were supporting her, she said. 'They are fine boys,' she told me. 'They give me everything I need—more than I need.'

"I felt sorry for the old lady, but I would have felt that way about anyone old and sickly. She was a complete stranger to me. She showed me pictures of her four sons, their wives and their children. She said they were all doing well and had beautiful, smart children. Thirteen of them, she told me. It nearly blew my mind—those kids are my nieces and nephews! Can you imagine that?"

Rick gave a long, low whistle and for a few seconds seemed far away. Then he got back on track and started talking again.

"She wanted to know if I wanted to meet my brothers, but I told her no, and I think she was relieved. She said, 'What's past is past. Let sleeping dogs lie.'

"I got home all worn out and my folks didn't hassle me about where I'd been or why I had used up all my money. They were really glad to see me. Now we're talking about training me to help out with my dad's business."

"Wow! That's some story, Rick!"

They were silent for a moment. David's mind was in a whirl. What if he were to search when he was eighteen? What if . . . what if . . . David pulled himself together from thoughts of the future to the excitement of the present.

"How do you feel about going into your father's business, Rick?"

"Great! Only I'm not going to be a pussycat like my dad. I mean, as far as my mom is concerned. He's great in the business. But in the house he's just a zero without the circle around it! Mom bosses and nags him all the time. I think she's really mad at him because she is sure his folks are disgusted with her for being 'barren'—that's the way she talks about herself. I've never heard anyone else call her 'barren!' Can you imagine anyone taking it so hard just because they couldn't have babies?"

58

"Yes, I can, I think I can," David answered. "I guess some people make the best of it."

"Maybe that's why my mom was so bossy—and on all those boards and things, and such an expert on 'learning disabilities.'"

Hmmm," David murmured, half to himself. "But Rick, maybe she was just naturally like that . . . take my mother. I know she felt bad about not being able to have a baby with my dad. No, positively, she's not bossy."

"Yeah, well . . . people are different, I guess."

Rick picked up his jacket and began to put it on.

"Don't go yet, Rick! I want to hear about Beth and Rachel and Ellen."

"Not today. It's after four o'clock already, and I'm going to get caught in the heavy traffic and ride in a loaded bus as it is. Tell you what, why don't you come over to my house one day next week? Come in the morning and we'll go to McDonald's or some place for a hamburger. I'll ask Rachel and Ellen and Beth to come with us. How about it?"

"Great! When?"

"How about Wednesday? My mom has a meeting on Wednesdays, so she won't be around to hassle us."

David's mother didn't seem too pleased when David told her he wanted to see Rick again. But she looked hard into his face and said, "I guess it will be all right."

"I can see that you're bursting with curiosity," she said at bedtime. "You can hardly wait for Wednesday to come around." She sighed and looked deep into his eyes. "I hope you're going to have a great time. Just remember, though, you're just fifteen. Rick is eighteen, and he may be doing a lot of things that you're not ready for!"

"Oh, Mom, you know I can take care of myself!"

"I trust you, David."

"I know."

When David told Diana about what he was going to do and about his mother's remark that Rick was doing a lot of things that he, David, wasn't ready for, Diana laughed.

"Your mother's not so dumb, David. She knows her son!"

15

Although it had only been five days since Rick had been over, it seemed much longer to David. Tomorrow's the day! he exulted. David's thoughts that night were of Rachel, Ellen, and Beth. Especially of Beth.

Beautiful Beth! In his mind's eye he saw her again— her straight hair a shimmering wave of black and the prettiest features David had ever seen—gray eyes, a lovely luminous pale face, and a luscious coral mouth. She was what David imagined a wood nymph might be like.

Beth was shy. But it was not the kind of shyness that made a person uncomfortable. Certainly not David! It made him want to take her by the hand and lead her wherever she wished. David wanted to comfort her, give her courage, love her.

David had fantasies about her that night. He recalled a ballet to which his parents had taken him. A beautiful girl had danced the part of a swan. Beth could easily have been that girl.

60

In his fantasy he danced with her. He leaped high into the air and twirled around her when he descended to the floor. He watched her with delight as she delicately went through her movements. Then he carried her high above him, across a stage which in his fantasy became a green meadow. There he drew her to him and kissed her shy mouth. He abruptly stopped his fantasy before the ballerina he had seen onstage drifted into the motionlessness of Death. But not before he had shed tears thinking of Beth—so shy, so afraid to get close to anyone.

Beth would be nearly fifteen now, just a few months younger than himself. What would she be like? Would he be able to talk with her the way he was able to talk with Diana? It would be wonderful!

Morning came—sunny and without a trace of smog. David bounced out of bed, showered and dressed hurriedly. His face was shining, his hair as much in place as he could get it. *Down boy, down,* he told the cowlick that insisted on standing up in his hair.

He bounded down the stairway and rushed into the kitchen. His father was not there.

"He's on the phone," his mother explained.

"Well, David," his father said as he came in for breakfast. David was already spooning up his cereal. "You've got a nice day for your outing with Rick. And it certainly appears that you are looking forward to it." He patted David on the shoulder and looked into his eyes for a moment before he, too, sat down to breakfast.

Rick and Rachel were at the bus stop when David stepped onto the curb.

"Hey, man! You made it," Rick said.

Rachel threw her arms about him and kissed him heartily on the lips, holding him so close that he could feel her breasts. WOW! There he was, getting all gooey inside.

"Where's Beth? I thought she'd be with us."

"Naw, my mother wouldn't let her come."

"But . . . but why not?"

"Rick, you'd better tell him why. He'll understand. He's one of *us*, you know."

What did Rachel mean? Why those funny looks she and Rick were exchanging? He found out soon enough, too soon for his peace of mind.

They were no sooner seated at McDonald's when Rachel said, "Well, when are you going to tell him?"

"Now don't take it too hard," Rick warned.

"Take *what* too hard? Come on. Tell me, tell me!"

"Take it easy, kid!"

"Well?"

It was Rachel at last who told him. "Beth is pregnant."

David's mind went blank. Rick squirmed in his seat.

"Gawd, David, don't take it so hard. I've been pregnant, too. It's not such a heavy thing, you know. It happens all the time!"

"Shut up, Rachel! Can't you see how flipped out he is?"

David moaned. At last he was able to speak.

"How did it happen? Was she raped or something? She didn't just *let* him, did she? Who was it? What is she doing about it?"

"Hold on, hold on. Everything is going to be all right."

"How CAN it be all right? Is she going to have an abortion?"

"No, my mother's taking her away, and when they come back, they'll meet us in South Carolina. They'll say they had to arrive later because *Mom* just had the baby!"

"You've got to be out of your mind, Rick! How can she pull off a stunt like that?"

"Mom thinks she can—and when my mother thinks she can do something she generally does it! She's wanted to have a baby ever since she got married. NOW she's pulling it off! Won't she lord it over her sisters-in-law!"

"Can I see Beth? I must see her . . . please?"

"No, my mother doesn't want me to bring you

around. She's not taking any chances on anyone finding out it's Beth who's having the baby. They're having it in Boston, where they don't know anyone. And when they get to South Carolina, it's Mom's baby, not Beth's."

"How did it happen? Was she raped? Who did it to her?"

"Do you have to know everything?"

What were Rick's shifty eyes telling him? Rick looked guilty. Was it possible? Could it have been Rick?

Rick guessed David's thoughts, and his eyes blazed with fury. "Idiot!" He spat the word out. "What kind of a mind do you have? Do you think I'd have done such a thing? To my own sister? What do you take me for?"

"How did it happen? Tell me," David pleaded.

"I'll tell you," Rachel said. "Rick was having one of his goofy friends over at the house while his folks were out. This guy talked Rick into going out to get some pizza, and when Rick got back, the creep was humping Beth like mad."

Rick lowered his head into his hands. "She didn't even try to stop him. She never learned to say no. She's just one of those kids with no mind of her own. It's all my mother's fault. She never trained Beth to think well of herself, or even to *think* for herself. And I used to hear her talking about Beth's mother having been only fourteen when she had Beth. I think she was sending out signals to Beth to do the same thing herself."

Rachel sighed, "I don't think Rick's so crazy to think that way. It could have happened just like that. Now in my case . . ."

"Yeah, what about your case, Rachel? You've been asking for it since you were eleven years old!" Rick sounded bitter.

Rachel shot him a disdainful look. Then she cuddled up closer to him. "Well, didn't you ask for it? Didn't YOU like it?"

"All right, all right. Shut up, will you?"

"Oh, you're ashamed to admit you got me pregnant, aren't you?"

"Only one of your pregnancies was mine. How many of them have you had?"

Rachel, tough kid that David thought her to be, was close to tears. "If you had two smart brothers and your parents, especially your dad, thought you would never amount to anything, and that you'd be just like he imagined your birth mother was, wouldn't you just go ahead and make the best of it, have a little fun and hurt your father as much as you could?"

"Listen, Rachel, I'm sorry." Rick looked shamefaced, then put his arm around Rachel and squeezed her. "You're a great kid, you really are. And I don't think your folks are that bad, either. They've stood by you. They haven't given up on you. They care a lot. I think they really love you. And you know why they love you? Because you're a great girl, that's why!"

David, with an effort, pushed aside his sorrow and concern about Beth. He looked long and hard at Rachel. She really was OK. She had what his mother had once described as "warmth and vitality."

Thinking of his mother and how she might worry, David said, "I ought to be getting home soon. But I was hoping to see Ellen, too. What's happening to her?"

"She's OK," Rachel answered quickly. "Her folks don't want her to see me anymore. They think I'm a bad influence. And I guess I really am. She was out with me one time when the cops picked me up for speeding. They called her parents and told them that I didn't even have a license to drive. I didn't get her into any real trouble. But that was enough for her mother to order her not to see me any more."

David's mother knew something was wrong as soon as David walked into the house. She pulled him close to her and rocked him in her arms. Big as he was, he submitted to her tenderness and felt comforted. He would have liked not to feel like such a big baby.

David told his mother all that had happened. She

64

took it all right, murmuring something about Beth and a "self-fulfilling prophecy."

"And don't worry about Rachel," she said. "She'll turn out OK. You'll see."

David wished his mother would say the same thing about Beth, but she didn't. Poor Beth. He thought he understood what his mother meant by "self-fulfilling prophecy." He recalled that Rick had said something about his mother's fearing that Beth would repeat her birth mother's pattern. Was it deep down something that she really had wished all the while she was "protecting" Beth? Was Beth's mother really giving her mixed messages?

David thought of Beth that night. She was again the dying swan of the ballet. He carried her to the lake and gently placed her on the water. They both sank down together as wave after wave washed over them, and David fell into a deep sleep.

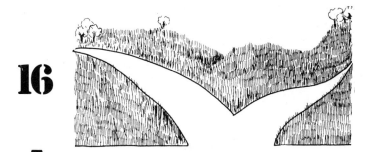

16

Adam, Chris and David had not known each other before they met in the group, nor had their parents known each other. But the parents had taken such a liking to each other the first time they met in the group that they had become friends. When the Termans moved into the Brooks's neighborhood to be close to the high school they wanted Adam and Chris to attend, David began to see more of the boys than he saw of any of the others who had been in the group with him.

He did not particularly like Adam or Chris, but the closeness of the two sets of parents, and the short distance between their homes, brought the boys together. As time went on, David found himself intrigued by the differences in their personalities.

Adam kept to himself a lot and wasn't particularly friendly. Chris, on the other hand, was a wise guy, and he was always making jokes and bragging. He messed around in school and often made a nuisance of himself, but he still got good grades.

The teachers liked Chris despite the disturbances he frequently created. David guessed that being good-looking and bright helped. Chris, moreover, had some of the qualities that used to attract David to Jason Cummings. David got a kick out of Chris's devilishness, and he wished sometimes that he could be more like Chris. But he contented himself with enjoying Chris's antics without having to deal with the consequences.

"Guess what happened today in school," David said to his parents at dinner one evening.

"What now?" his father asked.

"Well, Mrs. Halloran—she's our math teacher, you know—let out a big scream when she sat down at her desk this morning. Then she held up a tack that had been on her chair. She was the only one who didn't suspect it was Chris who had put it there. And Chris was the only one who didn't giggle or even try not to! He just sat there looking like an angel. Mrs. Halloran knew there was no use trying to find out who did it, so she gave us all an extra assignment for our homework."

His mother shook her head and looked sad. "Ruth and Ted had a lot of courage to take on those two boys," she said.

"What do you mean, Mom?" David loved to hear his mother analyze things.

"I don't know who to feel sorrier for—the Termans or the boys. Adam was two-and-a-half years old, and Chris only fourteen months, when the Termans took them into

66

their home. I'm sure they must have had some terrible times before they were placed with the Termans."

"Yeah, they told us all about it in the group. Their mother walked out on them. Their father took them all over the country, coast to coast, trying to find their mother or the grandparents, or any relatives who would take care of them."

His mother sighed.

"But they have a good home now, so why do you feel sorry for them?"

"Well, David, you know how strongly I feel that the past is part of the present. I don't mean it in the way that Beth's mother did. Beth's mother actually thought that Beth might take after her birth mother, who got pregnant at age fourteen. That's just silly.

"What I mean is that a person's experiences leave 'creases' on the brain. That's what you've called them, David—'creases.' Adam at two-and-a-half years of age might even have had some actual memories of the difficult times in their first home. Even Chris, at fourteen months, may also have had some vague or distorted memories. In any case, the children did not have a 'good start,' as babies do when they are born—or adopted early—into good homes."

"You mean they were sort of 'damaged' when they were adopted?"

"Something like that, dear, but that doesn't mean it needs to affect them the rest of their lives. But the past is always in a way part of the present. It means that the Termans would have had an extra hard job in making the boys feel loved and wanted."

It was not long after that conversation that David heard that Chris was disturbing his classes to the point where the teachers, despite the fact that Chris was a good student, were getting impatient, and they thought that Chris should see a psychiatrist. David's mother thought Adam was the one who should see a psychiatrist. He was too quiet—"strangely quiet"—she said. Adam's mother told

David's mother that every minute Adam was at home he listened to tapes of rock music. The music was unbearably loud. Sometimes his mother reached a point at which she couldn't stand the noise anymore and yelled at him.

David's mother thought Adam's obsession with rock music was understandable. "It's a kind of symbolic search for his father—at least an attempt to identify with him," she said. David wasn't sure he understood exactly what his mother meant, but he got the drift of it. Adam was trying to be like what he imagined his birth father was like.

Adam went to every rock club that would let him in, and he spent hours watching "M-TV." After a while he even began to dress like some of the members in rock bands. He cropped his dirty-blond hair so short that it stood up in bristles, and he put an electric-blue zigzag where his part should have been. He wore a paperclip in his right ear, which was pierced, and wore ripped, skin-tight black jeans. But his speech didn't match at all. He had a thin voice and there was nothing rough in his manner or the way he talked.

Then something happened that changed Adam's and Chris's life for the better. David got the story piecemeal, partly from overhearing his parents talk when they didn't realize he was listening, and directly—also piecemeal—from Adam and Chris.

What happened was that Adam and Chris's birth father came to town and headed straight for the Children's Service Bureau. He met with Mr. Perkins and Mrs. Nelson. Mr. Perkins contacted the Termans, who agreed that the birth father could see the boys.

The reunion really settled matters for Adam. He never said much, but it was clear that he changed after that. And so did Chris. The boys were disappointed in their "real" father, as they often referred to him. He even tried to borrow money from the Termans, claiming that he was temporarily out of a job.

Adam and Chris had been expecting a sentimental reunion, but this man was a stranger, more interested in himself than in them. It was clear that whatever he felt was not "love."

The things he told Adam and Chris and the Termans were hard to believe. Maybe the boys didn't want to believe them. He claimed that his wife—the birth mother of Adam and Chris—was too immature to take responsibility for the children. Their little apartment had been full of dirty diapers. The beds always were unmade. Dishes piled up in the sink. According to him, their mother couldn't cook and didn't even try. They mostly ate out of cans.

"She was always crying," Ernie said—that was the name he went by. ("Ernie for Ernest," Chris said with a sneer, "and he was anything but earnest, though he sure tried to give that impression.")

"She was a real glamour girl, all right," Ernie told Adam, Chris and the Termans. "That is, when I first met her. She was a slob when she ran out on me and the babies. She left a note for me, saying the babies were with a neighbor across the hall. The note said she couldn't take it any more."

Adam looked crushed and embarrassed. Chris's lip curled in a look of disgust.

"Then what did he do?" David asked.

"Who knows what he really did?" Chris answered. "Would you have believed anything he told you? He said he tried to find her. He claimed he notified the Missing Persons Bureau. He even said he took us to the hick town where she came from, hoping her parents would take us. But they were dead. Nobody in town had seen or heard from her."

Adam shrugged his shoulders. "She probably died or something."

"I think she's probably hiding somewhere, scared that air head she married might be looking for her," Chris sneered.

The Termans did not believe in shutting out the birth father, but it was obvious that the boys disliked him. Contacts were sparse and limited. Ernie spent very little time with the boys, and he soon stopped calling them.

From that point on, Adam changed. He was no longer interested in being what he had thought his birth father was. His love for music remained, and his passion for rock led him to become the disc jockey for their high school dances. What had been an outlet for his anger became a way for him to feel connected with others.

As for Chris, he didn't settle down for a long time. And no wonder. Despite his pranks and inattentiveness, his teachers still liked him. He had the gift of a "silver tongue," Chris's dad called it. Or was it a curse?

"Things come too easy for him," David used to hear Mr. Terman say.

Mrs. Terman told David's mother that Mr. Perkins was arranging for Chris to see a psychotherapist through the Children's Service Bureau.

17

David took his College Board exams for the first time in his junior year of high school. What a surprise to find Philip at the testing center! He hadn't thought that Philip would be going to college—he certainly hadn't been headed that way when they had last met and when he had heard of Philip's living at Hillcrest.

At the end of the exam they both went straight toward each other. Philip was grinning from ear to ear.

"Hey, how ya doing, Davey?" he shrieked.

"Great! How about that?"

They looked for a vending machine, and each got himself a sandwich and a cold drink. They found a bench outdoors to sit on.

Philip talked of having been at Hillcrest and what it had been like living on the grounds in a cottage with others of his own age. He had stayed there for six months.

"It helped me," Philip said. "And it helped my mother even more. She would never admit that she was sorry she adopted me, and that was part of her problem. And of course it had a lot to do with my problems, too."

"Do you really think she was sorry?"

"I'm sure of it!"

David thought, How could Philip stand it?

"I was glad to get away when Mr. Perkins suggested that I live at Hillcrest for a while. My mother and Tom were getting meaner and meaner all the time, and it was getting harder and harder for me to take. Part of me was angry at them for not wanting me around. I was so goddam angry that I just about split my gut!"

Philip's face got red and his lips closed together in a thin, hard line.

"And I did things just for spite, because I was angry. I wanted to hurt my mother for loving Tom more than she loved me. I used to hit Tom. I wanted to hurt him. I was angry with him for being born to my parents and for *looking* like them!

"But all the things I was doing made my mother angrier and more disgusted with me. I was getting even, all right. But where was it getting me? What good was it doing?

"While I was talking to my psychiatrist and my social worker over there at Hillcrest, I heard myself saying a lot of things that really made me think. I learned a lot about myself.

"I suppose I could have learned some of those things

71

in our group—but I just didn't want to, I guess. Being away from home, and being with other kids who were having some of the same kind of problems—well, I guess that's what I needed in order to understand what I was doing to myself and to Tom and my mother.

"I began to see my mother differently. She misses my dad terribly. Maybe she even loves Tom more than she loves me because Tom looks so much like his father—and some of the love she felt for his father got 'transferred' to Tom— that's a word I learned from my social worker.

"My mother really had a rough time after my dad died. We all missed him, but it was different for her. First of all, she didn't know how to manage money. After she went through what my father left she had to go to work. She hadn't ever worked before, either, and she wasn't trained for anything. Finally, some fancy shop where she used to buy her clothes offered her a job as a saleswoman.

"She cried a lot after she came home from work—not only because she was so tired, but because her old friends didn't invite her to go out with them and their husbands any more. Some friends, huh?"

"That must have been rough on her!"

"Another thing—the fact that I looked different from my mother and Tom used to bother her a lot—it bothered me, too, especially after my father died. As long as he was alive, it was OK. He loved having me look like *his* brother, and he used to make a big fuss over me. But my mother wouldn't admit—even to herself, I think—that she hated my being so different-looking."

"That must have been hard to take."

"Yeah, it sure was!"

They talked some more, but about other things, about college and plans for the summer. They promised to get together again soon.

18

"**G**uess what?" David asked his parents at the dinner table after his meeting with Philip.

They listened attentively as David told them of his meeting with Philip, and were happy to hear how well he was doing.

"I had a feeling," his mother said, "that Philip would be willing to face up to his responsibilities if given some insight and encouragement."

"Which he certainly wasn't getting at home," David's father added.

"Philip thinks it bothered his mother to have him look so different from Tom and herself. Did that come out in the meetings of your group?"

His mother hesitated. She looked at her husband questioningly, and after a second's hesitation he nodded. "I can't see that it is breaking any confidence, nor can it do anything but good at this point for David to understand his friend—he already is quite aware of the problems Philip had."

"We were very sympathetic toward Philip's mother," she began. "We recognized what a hard time she was having, and we wanted to help her in any way that we could. I think in a way we did help her to see her own prejudice about Philip's looking so different from her and his brother Tom."

"How did you do that?"

"Mainly by listening and letting her express her feelings. At one point she blurted out quite angrily that she knew we were 'prejudiced' about Philip's looking so 'different' from the rest of our children.

"We didn't give her any argument. We just kept calm but probably showed in our faces what we were thinking. I think it helped her to become aware that she was transferring her own feelings, attributing them to us."

"Hmmm," David said thoughtfully. "That's a very interesting idea. I like Philip a lot. We're going to be seeing each other when we get the chance."

It was a long bicycle ride between Philip's house and David's, but they met two or three times before summer vacation began. They had wonderful talks in these visits. It was great to discuss each member of the group and the way they had learned to open up with each other, to listen closely and try to understand what really lay behind the words that were being spoken.

One day during one of their visits David asked, "Did you ever get to find out more about who your birth parents were?"

"Yes, my social worker at Hillcrest got some information. My birth mother was Anglo—very pretty . . . smart in some ways and dumb in other ways. She ran away and got mixed up with a crazy bunch of kids. She went in for drugs and stuff.

"They gave her psychological tests that showed she was 'gifted'—I guess by that they meant she was very bright. I must take after her, because I test out 'gifted,' too. Maybe even the birth father was—I sure must take after him in looks—in coloring, anyhow.

"All they could find out about my birth mother was that she was blonde and blue-eyed, and her name was Nancy something-or-other. She wouldn't give them her full name."

"Couldn't they have traced her through the Missing Persons Bureau?"

"No, nobody reported her missing. I wonder what

kind of parents she had. I suppose they don't even know they have a grandchild—ME!"

"What about the birth father. Does he know about you?"

"I don't suppose so. They said Nancy wouldn't even talk about him. Maybe she didn't even know if he knew. But I don't care—at least not very much. I'm going to make it for what *I* am."

David now rarely thought about being adopted. He was busy, happy and falling in love with Diana. They walked together to school every day as usual, sometimes openly holding hands. When they were alone with each other they often kissed, shyly at first, then more ardently.

He began to notice her breasts—those round, alluring protuberances that he longed to touch, but dared not. The way Diana looked at him sometimes, he wondered if she wanted him to do more than kiss her.

He wished that he could talk to someone about his feelings. Not his parents, of course. It would be just too embarrassing. He certainly didn't need to be told that he was too young to marry. Nor did he want to at this point in his life. He wanted to finish college, to have a profession of some kind, or at least to be trained for an interesting and responsible job. He knew he had some artistic talent, but not enough to become famous. And certainly not enough to afford a family for a long time, if ever.

In his fantasies he would be able to provide his family with a home at least as nice as the one he lived in now. He wouldn't need to live in as grand a house as Diana's— with a swimming pool and a tennis court.

Even if he could picture Diana living as modestly as his own family, he still had a long way to go before he could marry. And he would never, never give in to his feelings and do to Diana what Jack had done to Diana's sister, Emily. To have a baby before he could marry and provide a proper home for a family? NEVER.

At home he grew mopey. He ate his meals silently, responding to his parents only when asked a direct question. One evening his father abruptly asked him, "David, is there anything you would like to talk about, 'man to man,' so to speak?"

David felt his cheeks redden. He couldn't look his father straight in the eye. His father wouldn't understand, he thought. Besides, it would be too embarrassing.

Maybe he would get in touch with Mr. Perkins and see if there was some group where they could talk about such things in the way they had done at the Adoption Workshop.

One night, after they had gone to a particularly exciting and stimulating movie and he had taken Diana to her door, as he leaned toward her for their usual good-night kiss, a wild feeling came over him. He felt a whirring in his whole being. He wanted to hold Diana close, to surround her and be part of her, to make her part of him.

Then he felt a sudden anger. Were these the feelings his birth parents had experienced? Had they yielded to them? Had he been born of such feelings?

He turned from Diana and ran, not looking back. He was hardly able to insert the key in the door because of the tears that blinded his eyes and the rage that filled him.

David was looking forward to visiting colleges with his parents during the summer. The three of them discussed where they should go. David found himself deferring to his father, impressed with his acquaintance with many colleges. He became aware that his father, through a network of professional organizations and publications, knew a good many professors at various universities and colleges, as well as the kind of work being done, not only in his own field of economics, but in other areas as well.

David's father said a person could get a good education anywhere. It was what the student put into it that mattered most. When it came to choosing a university for graduate work there were other matters to be considered— but that would come up later.

Meanwhile, they were setting up appointments in advance for interviews with the admissions officers of the colleges that the three of them—David and his parents— decided they would like to visit. David knew his parents would send him to any school he chose. But he felt he should go to the college that gave him the largest scholarship he could get.

David's grades were good, and his advisers at school had assured him that he had little to worry about. But David wasn't going to depend on their assurances. He was going to make the most of his senior year and get the best grades he could. College Board exams would be coming up again in his senior year. If he could achieve even higher scores than in his junior year, it would be quite an accomplishment. And David felt confident about his personal record and his involvement in school activities. He felt happy that he was competing in an arena where being a rich kid didn't count for everything.

Since Professor Brooks would not be teaching during the summer, and was giving a series of lectures in the East, they would combine a summer vacation with a tour of colleges.

The three of them—David and his parents—took a plane first to Boston. When they arrived, they rented a car at the airport. On their first trip they drove through an underground tunnel. David found it a little scary to be closed in—"under the ocean," his father told him. When they emerged David's first impression was a "New England picture postcard," as he put it.

"This used to be 'Scollay Square' in my day," his father said. "It was a hangout for sailors and prostitutes. The shops were small and carried shoddy merchandise."

Now it was an area renovated in Colonial style, with government buildings and fascinating little shops. David's father was glad that Durgin Park, a famous old restaurant, still remained. They enjoyed a delicious roast beef lunch, with Dad talking nonstop about his old college days in Boston. He had expected to become an accountant, but on the way developed an interest in economics.

"How did you get into teaching?" David asked him.

"I had an economics teacher who thought I was OK. He made me an assistant, and he started me grading papers. Then he recommended me for a teaching position as an instructor at UCLA, where I've been ever since."

"And that's where you met Mother, wasn't it?"

"Yes. You must know the story by heart, the one of how we met in the bookstore. Your mother was a student in the art department at the university. She was browsing through the art books, and I found myself very much attracted to her. I had always liked red hair—and hers was almost as red as yours at the time."

"Did you get introduced?"

"No! It was a 'do-it-yourself' job!" He flashed a tender look in his wife's direction. She returned it, her eyes suddenly moist and her cheeks flushed.

David suddenly thought of them as both having once been young and feeling the things that he himself felt about Diana.

"Did you want a baby right away?"

His father answered. "We couldn't afford to have a family on an instructor's salary. So Mother finished school, took a job as an art teacher, and we tried to save enough for a house. By the time I was promoted to assistant professor we had saved enough money to put a down payment on our house, and then we tried to have a baby."

David noticed the tears in his mother's eyes. He wanted to ask whether they could have had a baby if they had not postponed trying to get pregnant until they could afford it.

David didn't have to ask. His mother, as usual, seemed to read his mind.

"If we had begun a family as soon as we married," she said, "which of course we were not in a position to do, we might never have had you, David. We would have loved to have had a child born to us, and we tried. We never found any reason we weren't able to—it just never happened. But no one I can possibly imagine, David, would be what you are, or mean what you have meant to us. Of course, we often wished that you could have been born to us. Maybe you wished that, too."

"Oh, yes!" Yes, yes, yes, yes, he thought.

They continued visiting colleges along the eastern coast, stopping for a day or two at the colleges at which David's father was lecturing, until at last they began to turn westward. There were so many colleges! David was glad he would have his father's help in choosing one of them—that is, if he had a choice.

It was a happy time for the three of them, and each experienced the intimacy, the congeniality and the joy of being together. For David, especially, the sense of two loving parents focusing upon him, helping him to plan his future, and giving him the freedom to express his own aims and ambitions was inexpressibly satisfying.

It was only when they were visiting Cornell, in Ithaca, New York, that David sensed a kind of restlessness in his parents. The campus was beautiful. The admissions officer was friendly and encouraging. So what was wrong? Why did he feel some kind of difference in the way his parents were reacting?

David heard his mother ask if they should have come here. Unaware that David was within earshot, she said, "I keep thinking that we'll run into someone with red hair, blue eyes and freckles. And I keep wondering if there are any relatives of David's still in this area."

"Nonsense!" his father answered firmly. "There are lots of people in this world with red hair, blue eyes and freckles."

But these remarks set David to wondering, too. Looking for people with red hair, blue eyes and freckles who resembled himself, he had to disagree with Dad. There were most certainly NOT lots of people with red hair, blue eyes and freckles!

They ended their tour of colleges back in California, with visits to Stanford University and the campus of the University of California at Berkeley.

It was reassuring to David to realize again that in applying to college he was in a situation where being a rich kid wasn't that important. (Except, of course, in relation to whether you could get financial aid from a particular college or not.) Nor did it matter to his parents or anyone else that he was adopted. All that mattered was being a good student and a well-rounded person.

"You're going to have a choice, David," his father told him. "So you had better be thinking what your first, second and third choices will be."

David thought it would be great to live in any one of those historic places in the East that he had visited, but he felt he didn't want to get too far away from Diana, his family and friends. Stanford and Berkeley would be much closer, and he could visit home more often. Staying in Los Angeles had a certain appeal, and he could cut that "umbilical cord," maybe just by living in a dorm at UCLA, practically in his own backyard.

21

The summer was nearly over when they returned home. The first person he called was Diana. She answered the phone herself.

"I've been sitting here waiting for your call," she said, teasingly.

Her greeting was warm. She was glad he was back. What had she been doing all summer? Playing tennis, swimming, getting to know Emily's little Bruce better. "He's getting to be fun," she told David, "and I'm really getting to like children, I'm discovering." Diana's voice contained laughter. He wondered about it.

"And what about you?" she went on. "How was your summer? Which college did you like best?"

"I'll tell you all about it. How about tonight?"

Diana seemed to hesitate for a moment, then agreed. Was she breaking another date to be with him? Was it jealousy he felt? Yes, it most certainly was!

When he called for Diana that evening, he felt all the old passion and longing for the touch of her. She was more grownup and beautiful than he had remembered.

Their footsteps automatically took them toward school, and they laughed at the ease with which they slipped into an old habit. Then they wandered onto the campus at UCLA and sat on a bench and talked and talked. Their closeness made David dizzy with longing to touch and hold her, but he felt in her a kind of aloofness that kept him from it. She had changed, somehow.

They walked over to 31 Flavors and had a gigantic fudge sundae. On the way home she told him that she had been seeing Alex Parsons.

"I was lonely while you were gone, and Alex kept after me to go out with him. Just movies and ice cream."

"Does Alex still drive his dad's car?"

"No, he has one of his own, a Porsche."

"Oh."

"We went to the beach a few times. But David, we're just friends. You were the one I was always thinking about."

Did she mean it? David wondered. He felt unsure of himself, uncertain of Diana's feelings for him. She seemed different. Had he changed, or had she changed?

"School starts on Monday, our last year in high school. Will we be walking together, Diana?"

"Of course!"

His passion for her quickened as she offered him her lips. With her breasts and her whole body against his, the wildness within him returned. The longing to hold her close, to be part of her and she part of him, was almost unbearable.

82

"Oh, David!" she murmured, "I really missed you!"

Diana *seemed* the same. But she was different. He couldn't put his finger on what it was that was different. But he knew that she had somehow changed.

22

Diana and David walked to school together as usual on the first day of their last year in high school. Nothing seemed changed on the surface as Diana talked on about the "fun summer" she had enjoyed while David was away. Oh, she had missed him all right! But most of the time she was "just having fun."

Now and then Alex Parsons's name slipped out as she commented about a movie that she and Alex had seen together.

Diana was still chattering away when they reached school, and she scarcely had time to say, "Bye! See you at lunchtime" when a strong voice called out, "Hey, David."

David looked puzzled for a moment. Was this tall, rugged-looking boy with a deep voice the same, the very same person that David had known three years before in the group at the Children's Service Bureau?

"Hey, Carl!" David threw his arms around him and gave him a bear hug.

"You sure have grown, Carl."

"In what way?"

"You tell me, Carl." David laughed, thinking that "Mr. Freud," as the group had called him in their first meeting, was sure to come through in his typical manner.

"Yeah," he said. "I don't make trouble for my folks anymore. And I don't fight with other kids. Even the teachers like me."

"How come? What did it?"

"Oh, I guess . . . well, you know how I used to feel funny about being adopted. After the kids at school found out about it they used to tease me. I wasn't going to let them pick on me. I was going to show them a thing or two! And I did! I fought with anyone I even suspected might be thinking about my being adopted. I really hated the kids who said my 'real' parents didn't want me.

"Then I thought about the group. I thought about you, David. You never seemed to let it get you down. And I said to myself, 'Hey, Mr. Freud, what's the matter with you? You're nice. You're good-looking. You're smart!' Anyhow, I started to act friendly. And you know what? The guys were a little suspicious of me at first, but then they were OK. And the girls, too. I got to be friendly with some of them. I stopped making trouble for my parents—sometimes I think I was trying to make sure that they really weren't sorry they adopted me."

Carl and David became close friends despite the difference in their ages. Carl came over to the house a couple of times a week. They studied together, talked about experiences that had hurt them and those that had made them feel good.

David's parents enjoyed having Carl around. "It's almost like your having a younger brother," his mother said. "I'm so glad."

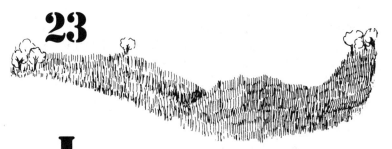

23

It was a busy year for David and an important year, with College Boards looming again and an avalanche of studying to do. Added to these responsibilities, he was on the soccer team and was art director for his class year book. He no longer felt friendless.

The only person who didn't seem to like him—and whom he didn't like—was Alex Parsons. He never forgot Alex's response when he had learned that David was adopted. "Yuck, you mean your 'real' mother gave you away? She didn't want you?" The words—and the tone in which Alex had said them—still hurt.

But David had to admit that it was more than that particular memory that caused his dislike of Alex. He recognized in Alex a competitor for the attentions of Diana—Diana was a friend whom David *could* not, *would* not share with Alex Parsons. Alex wasn't good enough for her! And besides, Diana was his own closest friend, and something more.

David's walks to school with Diana were more than the comfort to him that they had been when they were little children. He knew now that he was in love with her. Early in the school year he had already asked her to commit herself for the Senior Prom. He dreamed of her at night. He spent most of his free time with her.

David was sure that Diana liked him better than she liked anyone else. She was always reassuring him that this was so. But now and then he sensed in her a disturbing thought that she occasionally expressed.

"David, you're wonderful. You know there's nobody in the world that I like as much as you. But . . . I don't know. You'll be going off to college, meeting other girls. And anyhow, you and I are going in different directions."

"How do you mean that, Diana? You know I love you. I'll always love you."

"I'll always love you, David. But . . ." She seemed unable to finish the sentence.

"Do you mean because I might go away to college and you're not? What difference will that make? Even if I go East I'll be home for vacations. If I go to UCLA, I'll be right here!"

"That's not the point, David . . . our lives are going in different directions . . ."

"You already said that. What do you mean?"

"I don't know how long I want to wait before I can have a true commitment with someone. It's important for me to know that I can count on someone to be there for me."

"You won't wait? Just a few years?"

"It'll be more than a few years. You'll want to get into some profession, like teaching, or law, or medicine."

"Or psychology, that's what I'm interested in. Maybe I'll teach and write books—if I'm smart enough."

"Oh, you're smart enough. But I . . . well, I guess I'm comfortable with myself as I am. And I like the way I live now. It will be years before you can marry, and even more years before you'll be ready to have a family."

David did not respond. His face, though, showed his disappointment. And his hurt.

He thought of the difference in the way Diana's family lived, and the luxuries they seemed to need for their enjoyment and even happiness, as compared with the simplicity of his own family's life style and the things that gave them pleasure.

Diana's comments about Alex Parsons also came to mind. Alex was a real entrepreneur and was already planning a business that he wanted to work at full time. He was going to stay in town and go to school part time.

Aloud, he said, "You mean that you may want to marry Alex Parsons?"

"I didn't say that, David. It's you I love."

"Would you marry someone like Alex Parsons?"

"Maybe. He's not so bad. He just didn't understand about adoption at first, but he does now. He thinks you're OK."

"I guess you're right. I'm not ready to get married. I want to study and decide later on what I want to spend the rest of my life doing. And I'm not going to be ready to do that for a while."

They both became silent. Diana reached up and put her hand against his cheek. He could not respond. It will be years, he was thinking, before he could marry and have a family—to say nothing about whether he would ever be able to provide Diana with the things she enjoyed.

They did not discuss it again, but it never left his mind that someday he would lose Diana. Meanwhile, David allowed himself fantasies of love and marriage and a family with Diana at his side. They continued to kiss and hold each other close, to feel the way they wanted each other.

David suspected that he could have gone "all the way," as he had heard it called. Something always stopped him—perhaps the realization of how he himself had come into the world. Diana seemed readier than he. In fact, at times she was so provocative that he could hardly bear it.

Painfully, he would make himself remember some of the things they had talked about in the Adoption Workshop. And whenever he saw Bruce when he called for Diana, he would say to himself fiercely, "Never, never will I forgive myself if I am responsible for bringing someone into the world I cannot raise as my own child!"

24

Just before Christmas, David received a letter from Rick, with a postscript written by Rachel.

Dear David,

Are you sitting down? Get yourself a safe place, because you might just fall over when you hear the news! Rachel and I are married! No kidding! You know I've had a crush on her ever since we met in the group. I talked her into settling down with just ME! And now she's MY woman!

I'm in my father's business now, and he thinks I'm doing a good job. At least he doesn't complain. Once in a while, when he's very tired or Mom has been nagging him and he feels he needs to get away for a day or two, he even tells me how glad he is to have me in the business!

I'm taking an evening course in accounting at the business school of the University of South Carolina! How about THAT!!!!

I keep pretty quiet in class because I want to learn. I really want to be a success and give Rachel a nice place to live.

ESPECIALLY AFTER WE HAVE OUR BABY!!!!!

Yes, Rachel is pregnant, and my mother is in seventh heaven. Sam, or Susan, whichever it's going to be, is going to have a nice playmate in Lance, which is the name my mother gave "her" baby!

Beth is OK. She has a lot of responsibility for Lance, because my mother is too old and too tired to run after him all the time. Lance gets into everything and makes her nervous. (And now he's only crawling—can you imagine what he'll be like when he starts walking?) All the same, my mother is so proud of 'her baby' that she can't stop telling the world how smart and wonderful he is.

So what's new with you, kid? Please write.

RICK

And Rachel's postscript:

Rick and I are so happy, David. I'm glad to be away from my parents and my smart brothers. They were too much!! But I love them and appreciate all they did for me, and the way they put up with me.

You'll be happy to know that I'm not a "bad girl" any more—I don't think I ever really was. But I never felt loved unless I was having sex. Isn't that strange? Maybe your mother will understand. I think you learned how to analyze these things from her.

Anyhow, now I feel loved *all* the time! I think I was just meant to be married and have a baby of my own that I could *keep!*

Come see us. South Carolina is a great place to live, and Rick is a wonderful husband (and lover)!

RACHEL

David's mother was happy to hear the good news about Rick and Rachel. "I always did think Rachel would turn out all right. She was in a pretty difficult place at the time she was in the group.

"Life can be pretty tough for someone who's in the

89

'wrong' family. I mean, even if Rachel had been born into her family, her brothers still would have been a lot of competition for her. As it was, being adopted made it just that much more difficult for her."

That evening Mrs. Brooks went into David's room for their usual good-night talk. David sensed that she had something special on her mind, and he waited expectantly.

"David," she began. Her voice was somewhat hoarse, and this, too, was unusual. She paused to clear her throat. "David, I think you may feel a little more kindly about Rick's mother if you know the truth about her."

She paused again. What was she going to tell him, he wondered.

She spoke with more assurance as she continued. "After our last meeting Rick's mother asked me if I could stay for a few minutes while she talked with Mrs. Nelson, as she had arranged to do before the meeting began. So while Dad visited with Rick's father, I stayed behind with Mrs. Nelson and Rick's mother—her name is Pam.

"Pam said she wanted to talk with us about a very confidential matter. She had a high opinion of Mrs. Nelson's experience, and she felt that I was an understanding and sensible person.

"She told us that even after adopting Rick they still tried to have a baby. Just before adopting Beth, she went to an infertility clinic, which found no reason for her not having a child. She assured them that she knew all about trying at the right time—you know a woman is only fertile during a few days each month.

"They surprised her then by asking her to bring in a specimen of her husband's sperm. When they asked her a few days later to bring in another specimen, she became suspicious. This time they asked her to wait while they did some work in the laboratory. Then the doctor called her into his office to tell her there was no hope of a pregnancy. They could not tell her what caused the condition—but her husband had no living sperm, and even those he had were abnormal in shape.

90

"Pam cried as she told us what she had decided. 'I know my husband well enough to feel it would be a great shock for him to know the truth. It would destroy his sense of manhood. It might cause him to lose confidence in himself, and even affect his work, which he's very capable of handling. He's been pushed around by his mother and sisters. It's hard enough for me not to push him around. Am I doing the right thing not to let him know?' "

"So what did you tell her?" David asked.

"I don't believe she was really asking us what to do, David. She obviously had already made up her mind and just wanted to feel that we understood and sympathized."

"Why did her sisters-in-law assume that Rick's mother was 'barren?' " David asked.

"It is an age-old myth that women are the infertile ones. Mrs. Nelson explained this to us. It is now known that infertility is roughly a 50-50 proposition—sometimes it is the man who is infertile, and sometimes the woman. There are instances in which it is not clear which partner may be infertile. And in some cases the cause of infertility can be corrected."

His mother saw the question in David's eyes and responded to it.

"In our case, David, we never found the reason for not being able to have a child. It is true that I used to feel flawed and imperfect because of not having borne a child. The medical studies we underwent did not reveal any reason for my not conceiving once we began to try. But after we had you we were so happy that you were our child. You have been everything that we desired."

David returned his mother's look of affection and joy. Then a look of concern came over his face.

"Do you think it was right for Rick's mother to keep that information to herself? And to take all that bull from her sisters-in-law?"

"We cannot always know what is right for other people. We often aren't sure what is right even for ourselves, David."

"I'm glad you told me, Mom." David lay back on his pillow. "It helps me to understand a lot of things."

Later that week Mrs. Brooks ran into Ellen's parents, and she told David about her conversation with them.

All the children were doing well. They were especially pleased with Ellen. Her schoolwork was improving and she was getting along with the rest of the family.

"Her parents told me," she said, "that Ellen especially likes visiting her adopted brother Donald, and they are thinking of taking him home now. He is doing better, and is able to say a few words, and Ellen feels that she can do wonders with him. She has so much love to give and so much interest in helping people, especially children."

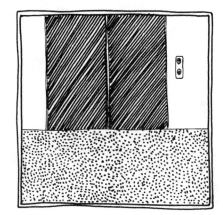

25

The night before his eighteenth birthday, David had a different kind of dream from the one that used to terrify him when he was thirteen.

In this dream he was in an ascending elevator. At first it shot up fast, then stopped suddenly with a jerk, and again sped upwards. The elevator swayed and lurched. Now and then the walls tilted toward him, then shifted in another direction.

The interior of the elevator was dark, but David began to make out a masked figure crouching in the opposite corner. He felt no panic, only immense curiosity about the figure. Was it a man? Was it a woman?

During one particularly violent lurch the figure in the corner came hurtling toward him. David rushed toward the center of the elevator. He caught it!

The elevator rose smoothly to the top floor, and David and the masked figure stepped into a pleasant, well-lit area. The mask slipped off. It was his mother! He put his arms around her and hugged her close. She smiled and began to croon a little rhyme that went:

> Where did you come from, baby dear?
> Out of the nowhere, into the here.

Br-r-r-r! The alarm rudely shook David back to reality. He awakened feeling wonderful. The old nightmare had been laid to rest. He now knew for certain that he had not been stolen. Mrs. Nelson had really "found" his parents for him. And certainly not the way Moses had been found in the bulrushes. But some day he, like Moses, might discover his true origins.

A delicious odor of breakfast was coming from the kitchen. David walked toward it, sniffing and chanting to himself the little rhyme of his dream.

"Happy birthday, David," his parents both sang out. The look his mother gave him was probably no different from the one she gave him most mornings, but he was more aware this time of her great tenderness.

His father put his morning newspaper aside. He looked at David with pride. "I'm very happy to have such a fine eighteen-year-old son. You've made these years happy ones for your mother and me. You seem especially happy today, too, son."

"I am," said David. "I think I finally understand something that's troubled me for a long time."

Then David described the nightmare that he used to have. "I used to wake up terrified, remember?"

"So that was it!" David's father was looking at him with astonishment and sympathy.

"You poor darling," his mother said. "If only you could have told us about it."

Then David told them of the dream from which he had awakened with such joy. He finished by crooning the little rhyme of his dream.

His mother looked surprised. "I used to chant that when you were a little tiny baby!" she said.

"I know," David answered. "It must have made some creases in my brain, where my memories are stored."

David hesitated, then blurted out, "I wonder if the agency knows more about me now, or could tell us more than they did then."

David's parents exchanged a knowing look. His mother said, "I think it might be a good idea if we all had a talk with Mr. Perkins. I'll call him."

David's father agreed with the suggestion. "Good idea," he said, after emptying his coffee cup with one gulp. He looked long and hard at David as he reached the door.

"I fully agree, David."

With a quick hug and wave to his mother, David also left. He was impatient to see Diana and tell her about the hope he had of finding out more about his birth parents.

It was a super day. Diana had wished him a happy birthday with a big hug. It had been wonderful to tell her that his parents were going to help him try to get more specific information about his birth mother than they now had.

"Do you think they may have a picture of her in their records?" Diana asked.

"I hope so! Wouldn't it be great to see what she looks like, at least!"

"Are you worried, David—I mean about what you might find out?"

"That, yes. But also . . . well, I wish I knew how she feels now about having given me away. I hope she's all right.

94

I wonder if she worries about me. I'd like her to know that I'm OK, and that I'm happy."

David hurried home after school. His mother's face told him that she had some news.

"Tell me, tell me! What did you find out?"

"A great deal, David. I'm so glad I called. Mr. Perkins told me that your birth mother telephoned this afternoon, as she does every year on your birthday! He explained that the reason he never told me this before is that it has not been agency policy to tell the parents up until now. I must say I was astonished to learn this.

"Mr. Perkins explained that the workers used to discourage birth parents from contacting the agency or trying to learn about the child they had relinquished. They felt it was healthier for the birth mother to put this entirely out of her mind—*as if she could!* They did not even encourage the adoptive parents to keep in touch with the agency until they realized they had an obligation to help the adoptive parents if they needed it. And, as you yourself have learned, they are offering adopted children some help in understanding and being able to talk about their feelings.

"Your birth mother is going to be here in Los Angeles for a home furnishings show, and Mr. Perkins was entirely willing to try to contact her with the idea of possibly arranging a meeting for you and Dad and myself to meet her. How about that?"

David grinned—literally, he could feel—from ear to ear!

"When? Where?" he asked.

"Mr. Perkins just called to say that he had arranged the meeting for a week from this Saturday. Your father is also pleased and thinks it is the right thing for all of us."

"How about THAT?" David grinned and leaped into the air, an acrobatic feat he repeated when he saw that they were eating in the dining room and that the table was set for *five* persons. Grandma Lola as usual would be present for his birthday dinner—and so would Diana!

26

David awoke to a glittering Southern California morning. A wind had been blowing during the night. He had heard it through his restless sleep as it swished through the trees.

Breakfast was earlier than usual, since their appointment was at 9:30 A.M. SHE was coming!

"She!" What was he going to call her? How do you do, birth mother? NO!

He showered in record time and flew into the kitchen. The odor of pancakes with maple syrup—David's favorite special breakfast—welcomed him.

There was little conversation at the table. An air of tension and anxiety hung over them as they ate. David's mother tried to fill the silence with chatter, but gave up after a while and tried to read her newspaper. His father barely skimmed the headlines as he turned the pages of his newspaper.

At last they left the house. David thought his father was driving more slowly than usual. Nevertheless, he noted that in just a few minutes by his watch they had reached the grounds of the Children's Service Bureau. They wound through the driveway. A few children were playing, roller-skating or tossing balls to each other. But there was less

96

activity than there had been when they had attended group meetings.

"Some children go home on weekends," his mother explained.

The main office building was silent. But the door of the Community Services building, in which Mr. Perkins now had his office, was opened wide. Through the windows, as they approached, David could see Mr. Perkins, Mrs. Nelson and—another figure! A kind of panic seized David—a panic mixed with the excitement of hope and anticipation—as he tried to make out something—ANYthing specific—about that figure.

Then they were at the entrance, where Mrs. Nelson was holding out a welcoming hand. Mr. Perkins rose from his chair to greet them. He waved his arm toward a seated figure.

"This is Susan," he said. "This is David. These are his parents."

Susan half rose from her chair, then fell back with a startled, incredulous look. She stared at David.

David returned her stare. The woman he saw presented an impression of a very different kind of person from his mother. He admired her appearance—hair, dress, makeup—all perfect, like a picture in a magazine or a commercial on television. A tantalizing odor of perfume surrounded her.

David felt somewhat overwhelmed by her poise and confidence—and aware that he was a little resentful of it. She just must be a selfish, unkind woman to be looking so self-assured when she had done such a terrible thing—given him away!

But when she spoke David felt less angry, for there was warmth in her voice and the glitter of tears in her eyes.

"I am Susan, David. I am your birth mother. I've heard many good things about you."

David sat there, wordless.

His mother broke the silence. "Susan, it has not been

easy for David to understand why you gave him up. His father and I do understand, and we are grateful to you for giving us the son we were unable to give birth to ourselves."

Susan leaned forward. She seemed to look deeply into Mrs. Brooks's eyes, and beyond them. "It's an ill wind, as they say, that blows no good. I'm glad that something good came of my misfortune."

David liked her words. They made him feel less angry toward her.

Susan turned to David. "The care I could have given you, David, would never have produced the young man I am seeing."

David looked back at her silently, with something of the resentment he was feeling showing in his face.

"I'm sorry, David. I was not able to be your mother. Please let me tell you why." She paused. David nodded.

"My father was an irresponsible, selfish man. He ran out on my mother and me. I was a 'latchkey child.' After school I came home to an empty house. The key I wore on a string around my neck opened the door to a silent, sad home. It was not the kind of home that I wanted for you. I wanted you to have the kind of home that I was always wishing that I had had, like the other children whom I knew at school.

"My mother was a filing clerk for a big insurance company. She might have done better for herself if she had not fallen in love before she finished her education. She left school when she was sixteen in order to marry.

"My father was too young for the responsibilities of marriage. He had no training or skills, and he found himself unable to earn a living. Straddled with a wife and child, he became discouraged and left us.

"Ever since I was a little girl I was determined to get an education and someday amount to something. Scholarships and part-time work got me through college. I am now what I wanted to be—independent and successful.

"It isn't that I didn't love you, David. When I first saw

98

you I was tempted to keep you. But when I held you in my arms and thought of doing to you what had been done to me, I said, no . . . NEVER! I know that in today's world some unmarried mothers manage somehow to survive. But I wanted more for myself, and for you."

"But what about my birth father?" David snapped. "Couldn't he have helped you?"

"He was putting himself through school. He was talented and wanted to be an artist. He took a full load of courses and also worked part-time. Art supplies are expensive, and he spent every penny he could save to further his work. I could not have interfered with his career. Besides, I knew that he would not have permitted me to."

Was it resentment that showed in her face? David wondered. Or was it sadness? Susan paused for a moment and set her mouth in a kind of determined line, then continued talking.

"We broke off our relationship then and there. He agreed that the best thing for me to do was to go to California and give birth to you, then place you in a good home through an adoption agency.

"He wrote to me in California for a time, but after you were born and placed with" . . . she looked at Mr. and Mrs. Brooks . . . "he stopped writing."

"Can you tell me something about him now?" David asked. "Is he a success?" His voice trembled. He wanted to hear that the man who fathered him was a world-famous artist, that his pictures hung in galleries. He recalled some of the modern paintings that he admired, and he hoped that his birth father had painted some of them.

"I think he is a good artist. But, as you probably know, success is not easy to achieve in that field. When I last heard of him he was teaching in the art department of a college in western New York, in the area in which both of us had once lived. Occasionally I see his name on an illustration of some article in a newspaper. They are very good, I think."

There was a moment of silence. David could not contain himself. He blurted out, "Do I look like him?"

The question startled Susan. She hesitated, and somewhat reluctantly said, "Yes. He has red hair, freckles and blue eyes. And a cowlick, like yours."

She looked at David hard and long, then shook herself, seeming to shrug off memories. When she spoke again, it was in a firm voice, as if she were speaking lines that she had rehearsed beforehand.

"I want you to know, David, that I think you are a lucky boy. I could not have given you the love and care that your parents provided. Sometimes I think that the hardships of my childhood have made me cold and unloving. Be thankful that I cared about you enough to want more for you than I could give you."

She got up and touched David lightly on the shoulder and began to turn away.

"Please!" he cried out. He couldn't let her go like that. His voice sounded strange to him—hoarse and scared. It felt as if a drum were beating in his chest.

"I think I would like to know you better," he said, "just as a friend and because—you know—all this business about roots and genes and stuff."

Susan hesitated. Then a soft look came into her face. "It isn't easy to give up a child, but I'm certain now that it was the best thing to do." She turned to David's parents.

"I don't have any right to a place in your son's life. But it has meant a great deal to me to know how things have turned out. I shall always care and be interested, and I am ready to be of help in any way I can if I am ever needed."

David persisted. "Or just to be a friend, to see you once in a while?"

David looked straight at his mother. He could see that she understood. His father didn't look too pleased. "We'll be in touch," he said crisply.

"There's something else that I would like," David blurted out. It took a lot of courage to say it, and his voice

100

shook a little and was hoarse. "Could I meet my birth father?"

Susan turned to David's parents, a question in her eyes. Mr. Brooks shrugged his shoulders. His wife nodded in agreement. David again felt a pounding in his chest.

"I haven't seen or heard from him for these past eighteen years," Susan said. "I think I can find out if he is still teaching where he was when I last heard."

"Would you prefer that we try?" Mr. Perkins asked.

"No, I think it will come better from me. I have some contacts who may know where he is. I'll try to get some information and let you know."

Susan's face looked softer, happier. She turned to Mr. Perkins and Mrs. Nelson. Her eyes were moist as she thanked them.

"And thank you again, Mr. and Mrs. Brooks, for all that you have done to relieve me of my concern for David. You have made it possible for him to have a good life, and I am grateful."

She nodded to David, her eyes filled with both pride and longing. David stepped toward her. He was aware that his resentment had eased. She had suffered, too. She had not just "thrown" him away.

He blurted out, "I will see you again, won't I? Just to talk, or maybe to be—what's the word you use, Mother?—to be acquaintances. Yes, acquaintances."

Susan turned toward Mr. and Mrs. Brooks. They nodded. Jonathan Brooks said, "He is our son. We have confidence in his judgment." He only slightly emphasized the word "our."

With a last lingering look at David, Susan left. There was contentment in that look.

David and his parents remained for a while with Mr. Perkins and Mrs. Nelson.

"Thank you for arranging this meeting," Mrs. Brooks said.

"It was good you were with us." Mr. Brooks added.

"Things might have gone quite differently without you."

"Oh yes," Mrs. Brooks added. "If David had had to do this in secret, without being able to share this with us, how awful it might have been!"

Mr. Perkins agreed. "The secrecy that has shrouded adoptions has not been good for anyone, even the *real* parents, yourselves."

"I wish all reunions could be like this," Mrs. Nelson said.

They parted. David felt emotionally drained and physically exhausted, but somehow elated.

27

Luck was on David's side—"deservedly," his parents said. He had a choice of several good colleges. It gave David a feeling of pride and self-worth to realize that he had been considered favorably.

At dinner, the three of them discussed the advantages—and disadvantages, if any—of each college.

David himself ruled out Cornell. "I don't think I would want to take a chance of running into my birth father," he said emphatically.

"What's your reasoning on that, David?" his father asked.

The question irritated David. Usually he welcomed this kind of discussion. It had grown to be a pleasant diversion—actually a habit that stimulated and stretched his mind. His mother described it as "serving up food for thought."

But this time David shrugged his shoulders. Out of the corner of his eye he observed his mother gesture to his father, a gesture that said as clearly as words, "Let it be!"

But his father did not let it go. "I suppose," he slowly said, "that if your birth father is teaching in the art department at a college in western New York State, the probabilities are that it might well be in Ithaca—at Cornell University or at Ithaca College."

"He didn't care about me," David said bitterly.

"We don't really know, do we?" his father answered.

David realized that his mother would like him to stay in California so that he could come home more often, or so that they could drive out now and then to see him.

"I think I want a change of climate," David said. "I liked the East. I'd like to find out if one of those schools will give me a scholarship before I decide."

"Good thinking, David!" his father said.

His mother looked a little sad, but also proud.

Prom night was coming up soon. Diana was to be his date. She had answered, "Of course," when he had asked her.

"That's great, Diana! I thought maybe you'd want to go with Alex Parsons. He'll be around next year, and you'll forget all about me."

"Oh, David, don't be silly. I go out with Alex Parsons because you're busy so much of the time."

"Is he really going to have his own business?"

"Yes. His father is giving him a loan. His dad is making a fortune, you know. Wanting to make money must run in the family."

A disturbing thought came into David's mind. Diana seemed so approving of Alex's being interested in becoming an entrepreneur and making money. Did that mean . . . ? He refused to think about it. And yet there was something he had to make clear, something that had to be said.

"You remember, Diana, that we said it will be years before I can marry and settle down. I want to be a doctor. Or maybe a psychologist. There's lots of medical stuff to learn just to be a good psychologist, but you don't need to spend all those years in medical school first."

"We'll see," Diana answered. Her voice was cool, but her eyes were soft and seemed to hold unshed tears.

28

Prom night! David had taken care to do all the proper things. Diana would be wearing a pink dress. He bought a white orchid with pinkish-purple markings to go with her dress.

Diana had said that her father offered to let David drive his car, but David had declined. "You don't mind going in our old Chevy, do you?" he had asked Diana, confident that she would agree. And she did, protesting indignantly, "What a question!"

David would be wearing a white suit, bought both for the graduation exercises and the prom. He packed his jeans and an old shirt in the trunk of the car because it was the custom of the graduating class to go to the beach after the prom and party all night. David had been careful to explain this to his parents a good two weeks beforehand, so that if they didn't like the idea he could work on them to accept it as the thing to do. And if his mother wanted to get a committee of parents to protest this practice—well, let her try. She'd have to learn that today's world was different from the one she grew up in.

On the way home from school he picked up the orchid and put it, box and all, into the refrigerator. He left a note to himself on the front hall table so that he wouldn't forget to take the orchid with him when he left to pick up Diana.

There was a letter on the table that he hadn't noticed when he had come in. It was addressed to him, postmarked Ithaca, New York. His hands shook as he opened the letter and read:

Dear David:

Susan wrote me and told me what a fine young man you are becoming. She said that I would be very proud of you.

She also told me that you would like very much to hear from me, and perhaps to see me.

David, some people might think me irresponsible and even a coward to have given you up at birth.

I do indeed feel irresponsible in having conceived you before Susan and I were ready for marriage and the care of a child. But I don't feel that I was irresponsible or cowardly in having given you up at birth.

Susan and I were convinced that we could not give you a good life. We could not have provided the care and upbringing and the opportunities that you deserved.

That's not to say that we didn't feel pangs of

conscience in having given you up. Susan must have felt this even more, carrying you within her as she did, doing whatever was needed to protect you and to give you good health.

I am sure she has tried all these years to harden herself against loving you and thinking about you. Her pride in you, and her seeing you as you are now, have meant a great deal to her.

It has meant a great deal to me, too, to know what a fine young man and gifted person you have become. You have had a home that Susan and I could not have provided. And even if we had tried, I believe we would have messed up your life pretty badly, given our immaturity, our lack of pre-paredness for responsibility and our eagerness to reach the goals that meant so much to us at the time.

I am married. We have a son. Right now I don't have the courage to tell my wife about you. Perhaps someday I can. Until then, I think it is best for us not to meet. If it should be possible at some future time, without bringing pain or conflict to you, your parents and my own family, I shall get in touch with you.

But when all is said and done, you—and you alone—are responsible for what you will become. I've met a lot of young people in my classes. Some of them are great, and some of them are just plain stupid. I don't mean that they have no brains or are unable to make something of themselves. They are just not ready to take responsibility for themselves. The ones that I consider great are those who know they are responsible for what they become.

I feel that I have failed you. But for God's sake, don't fail yourself. Good luck, David.

PAUL

106

David felt his head whistling, his heart beating faster, and his stomach churning as if he had an eggbeater inside. He went upstairs slowly to get ready for the prom.

29

David was dressed and ready to leave for the prom when his father asked him to come into the living room. He observed that his father was clearing his throat, as he usually did when he had something important to say. Especially when he was somewhat uncomfortable about saying it.

David waited. His curiosity to hear what was coming did not make him uncomfortable, as it had done when he was younger. His old self-doubts no longer troubled him.

"David, you know how proud I am of you. You are everything I ever wanted in a son. I wish your mother and I had conceived you, but I cannot imagine wishing for a son who would be in any way different from you."

Pausing, he seemed to be groping for words. That's a switch, David thought, good old Dad groping for words.

Clearing his throat, his father resumed, "The world is more accepting of. . . ." A frog in his throat stopped him, and while he was clearing it with one of his punctuated coughs, David wished that he could say the words that his father might be thinking, or actually put it to him this way: How about this, Dad? "The world is more accepting of illegiti-macy"—or of what they say in another way—"babies born out of wedlock?"

But David remained silent. Inwardly, he was aware of a kind of satisfaction, even of gloating. How often his father had made him uncomfortable!

"What I mean, David, is that kids these days are into sex a lot more than they were in my day. You yourself have had the experience of what it means to be born to young people who were not able to assume the responsibilities of marriage and a family. Er . . . do you know what I am trying to say, David?"

"I think so, Dad. You're trying to tell me not to get carried away tonight—sleeping out there by the ocean, with the sky and the moon above, right?"

"Not exactly, son. I'm trying to say that you should be prepared in case you ARE carried away! Do you know what I mean?"

"I think so, yes."

His father reached into his pocket and brought out a little packet that he handed to David.

"These are condoms, David. If you are carried away, be prepared. Don't think it's more romantic to be 'carried away' than to take the time to think of the consequences and to use one of these. Do you know what they are?"

"Yessir, I've seen them. I've never used them, or been in a situation where I needed them. But thanks, Dad, for being so understanding."

David felt himself getting red in the face. His hands were wet and sticky. "I don't know what will happen to-night, but I'd like you to show me how to use them, just in case."

That night, at the prom, David and Diana danced to-gether as much as Alex Parsons and a few others gave them a chance to do. Couples were always cutting in on each other, and David was not displeased when some of the cutting in was instigated by a few girls who wanted to flirt with him.

David knew that he would remember forever the night on the beach with Diana. He always would recall the pleasures of the warmth of the glowing fire, the companionship of friends, and the flavor of food and drink at two o'clock in the morning.

The ocean tides were strong. And the waves rhythmically pounded the shore, spraying white foam into the air and onto the sand. There was a crescent moon in the sky, but no stars. There were practically never any stars in Los Angeles, he thought dreamily, although sometimes a light twinkled in the sky that could have been mistaken for a star, except that it moved. Diana explained that the moving light was a police plane, looking for troublemakers and also making sure that none of the fires were out of control.

In the stillness of what remained of the night, couples gathered their sleeping bags and drifted off two by two. All that had happened contributed to David's anticipation and acceptance of what was to be.

The tumult of feeling and the joyousness both felt were far greater than had been described in any love story that he had ever read, or in any juicy description given him by others.

And, at last, too, David could understand, accept and forgive his birth parents for having yielded to desires that until now he had condemned in them.

30

It seemed to David that the summer passed unusually quickly before he went away to college. The love between David and Diana also quickened, and its sweetness was made more so by the inevitability of their approaching separation. It was painful for them to realize that they could not enjoy their present happiness much longer. On one evening shortly before David was to leave for school, they talked about it.

"David, you have to know that I'll miss you."

"I'll be back for Christmas, and spring and summer vacations, Diana. I love you. I don't want to face a future without you."

"David, I want to go on living the life I already have, the kind of life I enjoy. And I want to share it with someone who's ready for me now. You are living for the future. And your future will take you away from me."

"Don't say that, Diana. I don't want a future that doesn't include you. I love you. That will never change."

David truly felt that way about Diana. Yet he also knew that he was heading into a life in which his only certainty was the knowledge that he wanted to achieve something worthwhile for himself—and for others, too.

He felt he knew who he was now. The direction his

life was to take seemed clearer to him, even though his ideas about what he might do were not fixed.

How had he come to this point? He continued to try to understand. How had he survived the fears and doubts that had so troubled him? How had he overcome his perplexity about his origins, his concern about the mystery of his birth? It was in his nature to want to understand fully.

David's parents had an open house for family and friends on David's last evening at home. It was a joyous and exciting occasion, a celebration, David felt, on his having passed a major hurdle in his life.

Looking around after everyone left, his mother sank into a deep chair and stretched her feet out in front of her.

"This room is a disaster," she said.

David looked around and had to agree. It really was a mess. The furniture was out of place. Remains of food and beverages were strewn about the living room, the dining room, kitchen and even the entrance hall. David felt overwhelmed and exhausted.

"Don't bother about any of this, David," his mother said. "Your father and I will take care of the worst of it and put away the perishables. You probably have some last-minute things to take care of. In any case, get to bed as soon as you can—you have another big day ahead of you."

As David dragged his feet upstairs, his mother called out, "Let me know when you're ready to be tucked in."

The ritual of "tucking David in" had taken place for as long as he could remember. He would never grow too old for it, he thought, at the same time he realized that an era was about to end, the era of his childhood.

How long ago could it have begun? There must have been some little ceremony around bedtime long before his conscious memory could recall. His first memory was the finger play—"this little piggy went to market. This little piggy stayed home . . ." Things like that. There were songs, too, and other rhymes and poems.

He also remembered—with a deep sense of the pleasure and comfort it had given him—the way his mother had stretched his arms and legs and patted his back a little roughly, the way a masseuse might have done. All the while she had talked and sung.

As he grew older, there were stories, then books that she had read to him. Then he was the one who had read aloud, although often he would get sleepy and ask her to finish the story while he snuggled into his pillow. Sometimes he was asleep before she left. Other times he was not ready to let her go. Especially when he was little—maybe two or three years old. Sometimes she would give in to his pleas and sing something soothing until he was ready to sleep. Other times she would say in a firm but soft voice, "Now that's enough! Don't be such a tyrant!"

When that happened he would call her back, saying he was thirsty. She would bring him some water, urging him not to drink too much. And he soon learned that if he had too much at bedtime he would awake with wet and uncomfortable pajamas.

So he stopped that. Instead he would call her back, showing her the glass of water and telling her it was "too salty." She would explain to him gently that the bubbles in his water were from the water standing too long in the glass.

"Get to sleep, dear," she would tell him softly. But if he persisted, she would sometimes get cross and scold him. Soon he began to realize that this made her tired, and he did not want to hurt her.

His thoughts turned to Diana. He had walked her home after all the guests had left. Their parting had been poignant.

"Nothing will ever change my feelings for you," he had said. And she had assured him, in her practical yet tender manner, "You know that I care about you, David, but who knows where our lives will lead?"

David recalled his experiences in the adoption group, remembering how alone in some ways he had felt before he had met other adopted kids. In his mind's eye he again saw

Rick and Rachel, Adam and Chris, Ellen, Philip, Carl, and beautiful Beth. He would never forget them. He would always, he hoped, keep in touch.

He thought of all the influences in his life—of Susan and Paul, who had created him and still cared in their own way. Of his parents, who had nurtured and guided him. Of Mr. Perkins and Mrs. Nelson, who had undertaken the awesome responsibility of choosing his real parents. Of the group members, who helped each other understand and accept being adopted in a world that did not always know how to deal with adopted persons.

He thought of the future, of the new life he would have, of the opportunities that lay before him.

He opened the leather-bound diary his mother had given him to take to college. Its empty pages seemed to say something to him: Fill your life. Tell me its meaning. Point out your direction.

He picked up his pen and slowly, in a firm hand, he wrote:

> What is really important is for a person to realize that he can't go around blaming others for what he becomes.
> The way I see it is this:
> My birth parents gave me
>   the gift of being;
> Mom and Dad gave me
>   the opportunity of becoming.
> I CAN become the person I want to be. If I try. Whoever I am and what I will become is up to ME! I am myself, DAVID.

Acknowledgments

I am grateful to Gloria Smith, Reuben Pannor, and Janet Gast for their encouragement and assistance in the first stage of writing this manuscript, and especially to Gloria Smith for her continued supportiveness and devotion in following through to the very end of its preparation.

Special thanks go to Carl Schoenberg, Senior Editor of the Child Welfare League of America, for his encouragement and his suggestions throughout several rewritings of this manuscript, and to Alice Misiewicz, for the final editing.

Thanks are also due Samuel Berman, Director of Vista del Mar Child Care Service, for his assistance in bringing my manuscript to the attention of the Child Welfare League of America.

And who is Evelyn?

Evelyn Nerlove combined an urge to write with an ambition to pursue graduate studies. She received her M.S. from Simmons College School of Social Work in 1928. The desire to write, however, had to wait while she was employed as a social worker in Boston and Chicago, and while she and her husband, a professor of economics at the University of Chicago, reared three children, who have made Evelyn a grandmother of six. In Chicago, also, Evelyn Nerlove resumed work as an adoption specialist, and continued in the adoption field at the Vista Del Mar Child Care Service when she later moved to California. She has helped over 300 children into adoption and has continued to see many of them over the years. She pioneered groupwork both with adoptive parents and their children and continues to serve Vista Del Mar as a consultant, as well as conducting a private consulting practice. Evelyn Nerlove has of late nursed the latent creative writing spark into a small blaze of fiction-fact about adoptive life.

Who Is David? is one result. She cites Ann Morrow Lindbergh:

> The journey to find one's place in the world is the
> largest journey of all.

At 77, Evelyn Nerlove is still on that journey.